Where Should I Live
When I Retire?

A Guide To
Continuing-Care
Communities

Bernice Hunt

362.61 H939 wh
Hunt, Bernice Kohn.
Where should I live when I
retire? : a guide to
continuing-care communities
3 1120 03747 0969

SQUAREONE
PUBLISHERS

COVER DESIGNER: Jacqueline Michelus
EDITOR: Carol Rosenberg
TYPESETTER: Gary A. Rosenberg

Square One Publishers
115 Herricks Road
Garden City Park, NY 11040
(516) 535-2010 • (877) 900-BOOK
www.squareonepublishers.com

Library of Congress Cataloging-in-Publication Data

Hunt, Bernice Kohn.
  Where should I live when I retire? : a guide to continuing-care retirement communities / Bernice Hunt.
    p. cm.
  Includes index.
  ISBN 0-7570-0272-2
  1. Life care communities—United States. 2. Retirement communities—United States. 3. Retirees—Housing—United States. I. Title.

HV1454.2.U6H866 2006
362.61'0973—dc22

2005025308

Copyright © 2006 by Bernice Hunt

All rights reserved. No part of this publication may be reproduced, stored in a retrieval system, or transmitted, in any form or by any means, electronic, mechanical, photocopying, recording, or otherwise, without the prior written permission of the copyright owner.

Printed in the United States of America

10   9   8   7   6   5   4   3   2   1

Contents

For Morton,
my partner in everything

Introduction

This book is your complete guide to continuing-care retirement communities (CCRCs), the retirement option that eliminates concerns about long-term care and its financial burdens. A CCRC—or life-care retirement community, as they are sometimes called—enables you to continue your present independent lifestyle, but provides assisted living or nursing care on the premises if and when it becomes necessary. This book explains how CCRCs operate, what they offer, how they differ from one another, how to locate them, how to figure out which one is right for you, and how to proceed if you decide you want to live in one. But much more than that, this book also takes you through the psychological process of giving up the known for the unknown. Leaving one's familiar home and moving into a new community—that may or may not be as wonderful as the brochure says it is—can be an emotional and sometimes daunting experience.

So why do people move into continuing-care retirement communities? As you'll soon discover, there are many excellent reasons—long-term care foremost among them. You'll learn about the advantages and disadvantages of CCRCs and how you can avoid common pitfalls when making a choice. You'll also find out what to look for, what to steer clear of, what you have a right to expect, how to discriminate among various kinds of contracts, and how to make the transition when you move.

When my husband and I became interested in the CCRC concept in

1995, we had no idea how to get information. There was nothing in print that told us what we needed to know, and we spent a huge amount of time and money doing it the hard way. I would have given a great deal for a book like this one. That's why I undertook this project—to help you along your way.

The heart of this book is the account of the journey—psychological, emotional, and personal—that my husband and I took to get from our happy home in East Hampton, New York, to a continuing-care retirement community in a suburb of Philadelphia. It often felt like a journey to Mars. Your experience will, of course, be different from ours, but much of it will be similar. And I hope that at least some of the difference will have been made by the information you find in this book. I wish you a safe journey, with some fun along the way, and a happy landing.

CHAPTER 1

Crossing the Age Equator

Turning sixty-five is a little like crossing the equator. Whether it's one more day or one more mile, crossing to the other side has great significance. One doesn't suddenly become "old" instead of middle-aged, but a sixty-fifth birthday has special import. It bestows "senior citizenry," Medicare eligibility, and reduced-price movie tickets and bus fares. It's the time when many people retire and/or begin to receive Social Security payments. It is also the time when thoughtful children might begin to think seriously about their parents' future living arrangements.

My husband, Morton, and I sailed across the age equator with the greatest of ease. We were healthy, we were both working at careers we loved, we had just finished building a wonderful house, and our eighth grandchild was born even as the first ones were growing up and going off to college.

It was a happy time for us—but not for some of the couples we knew. One of our closest friends developed Alzheimer's disease, another Parkinson's disease, and yet another metastasized prostate cancer. We watched helplessly as these dear friends lost the ability to care for themselves. We did our best to support their care-taking spouses; we visited often, took them out to dinner, lent a hand when nurses got stuck in the snow, and shared their trials with them when a move to a nursing home became inevitable. We deplored the atmosphere of the nursing homes they wound up in—depressing places with rows of dull-eyed patients in the dayroom, staring blankly at daytime TV shows. Every time we visited, the same thought raced through our minds: *We don't want to wind up in a place like this.*

Looking back, it pleases me that we were able to look to the future in a clearheaded fashion; many people find comfort in blissful denial and just assume that the problems of old age will somehow take care of themselves magically so they can remain free of worry and get on with their lives. They may, from time to time, think vaguely that they will have to make some plans eventually—but not now, not yet. After all, everything is fine, isn't it? Why upset a perfectly good lifestyle before you have to? Meanwhile, their children may be doing a little thinking of their own. If they are in their forties or fifties, they probably have a few friends whose parents have suddenly run into serious health problems and need care. Even the most loving of children might be wondering if the need for a parent's daily care will erode their savings or if a grieving parent will need to move in with them and take over the guestroom they'd just acquired when their son finally moved out.

Just like their elders, adult children may also prefer denial to worry, but the likelihood is that they won't deny the need to make preparations for very long. There is too much at stake for all concerned. And so they gently begin to introduce a little reality—nothing too intimidating, of course, just a hint that maybe the house with its need for constant care could become a burden a few years down the road. It's useful for concerned children to do a little constructive research so that they have some attractive suggestions to offer. The more information they have, the more persuasive they can be.

Morton and I didn't need our children to get us thinking and moving. Life did it. Over what seemed like a remarkably short period of time, we lost several of our friends, even a few we didn't know were sick. We keenly felt the loneliness and isolation of our widowed friends, but we couldn't do much to mitigate it. When these friends began to have health problems of their own, they were virtually all alone.

Among our circle of "healthy" friends, cataract operations suddenly seemed to be in vogue. Arthritic knees kept so many of our former tennis partners off the court that it became difficult to arrange a doubles game. Myriad ailments turned up everywhere and, when possible, were laughed off. One friend quipped, "If you're over sixty-five and

A WORD OF CAUTION TO WELL-MEANING CHILDREN

If you are suddenly consumed with the need to get your parents to make some plans before it's too late, good thinking, but—whoa! Take it easy. Talk about it, sure, and tell them what you've learned, introduce some ideas, and kick it around, but don't be heavy-handed about it. If your parents feel they have been coerced into making a move will never be happy with it. Your aim should be to provide education and support without heavy pressure. If you use the Internet, there is a wealth of information available at your fingertips; useful websites can be found in the Resources section.

you wake up in the morning and nothing hurts, you know you're dead."

As time wore on, jokes like that began to seem less funny. Too many unfortunate things were happening to the people we cared about, and we realized that, inevitably, they would happen to us, too. We fantasized that we would both remain healthy and active, then die suddenly, without illness or pain, at exactly the same moment. But we knew that fantasy wasn't likely to become a reality. Still, we felt lucky because we weren't in crisis and had time to find and put a good plan in place before it was too late. And that seemed to be the key phrase: *Before it was too late.*

WHY ACT NOW?

While age is not a disease, it is a fact that the older we are, the more likely it is that our machinery will wear down, or that the transgressions of our youth (like indulging a passion for butter, steak, and ice cream, or smoking a pack or two a day) will finally catch up with us.

According to a U.S. Bureau of the Census projection, there are currently more than 5 million Americans over the age of eighty-five—that's an increase of 11 percent since 2000. Eighty-five-plus is the fastest growing segment of the population, and it's estimated that by 2030, there will be about 325,000 centenarians in the United States. Forty-four percent of Americans age sixty and over still had at least one parent alive in 2000—that's up from only 24 percent in 1940. (If you are middle-aged now, you can safely assume that at least one of your parents will be a part of your life for a long time to come.)

Why is this data important to know? One major factor is that, according to the Alzheimer's Association, about 3 percent of people between the ages of sixty-five and seventy-four have Alzheimer's disease (AD). While this may not sound like a lot, the risk increases steadily with advancing age: About 50 percent of the eighty-five-plus group is affected with AD. Caring for a loved one with this disease at home becomes ever more difficult and eventually becomes impossible. Almost all caregivers are eventually forced to find long-term care for their loved ones. (On average, people with AD live for eight to ten years after diagnosis, and can live for as long as twenty years.)

Alzheimer's disease is, of course, not the only worry of people in their advanced years. Many of the elderly who don't develop dementia become disabled as a result of cancer, stroke, osteoporosis, blindness, heart disease, or Parkinson's disease. And as a result, they too can no longer care for themselves. This is why it is so important that plans for long-term care be made well in advance, *before* any of these serious age-related problems crop up.

LOOKING INTO OPTIONS FOR LONG-TERM CARE

Giving up one's home to move to a retirement community is not the result of a simple decision; it requires a careful and thoughtful process that may take quite some time. So be patient—but do be sure to get an early start so that time doesn't run out. Life is full of surprises.

We knew we needed to plan for our future while we were still healthy enough to do so. We have wonderful, loving children, but they have their own lives, their own children, and their own careers. We didn't want them to be burdened with sick elderly parents, but most of all, *we wanted to be in charge.* We didn't want anyone else making our decisions, deciding our fate, or running our lives. We were used to being independent, to doing things our own way, and we weren't about to change—if we could help it. Realistically, we knew that whatever arrangements we made, we probably would not die simultaneously as we do in our fantasy. One of us would be left behind sooner or later, and another thing we knew was that we didn't want to rattle around all alone in a big house.

So what would we do? We began to review the options. Medicare does *not* pay for long-term care, and since some of our friends had been wiped out paying as much as $250 a day for nursing-home care (costs have risen since then), we looked into long-term-care insurance. Premiums vary depending on location and coverage, but in our state, New York, where costs are generally above average, moderately adequate insurance in 1995 was priced at $256 a month per person for those enrolling at age sixty and $454 a month at age seventy. Policies could be had for less, but they didn't cover enough to provide security. Some policies would pay $100 a day for up to two years—but $100 a day wouldn't provide the best facility, and what would happen when the two years were up? Also, no matter how much a policy allows per day, that sum will buy less and less in services as the years pass. So, for a long-term-care policy to be worthwhile, it must include inflation protection. Obviously, the best policies cost the most money, and however good the plan, the payoff is still a nursing home or the isolation of home care. Neither seemed like a good solution to us.

Of course, as in all areas, someone eventually builds a better mousetrap, and if you have enough money, you can buy one. A nursing home, built in Houston in late 2000, offers all the amenities of a luxury hotel right down to rooms of up to 560 square feet with mini refrigerators (stocked to your specifications, of course), an air-conditioned pet kennel, a playground for visiting grandchildren, and in-room high-speed Internet access. The price tag for a top accommodation in the opening year was $11,000 a month. One could probably be reasonably comfortable here, but your average insurance policy wouldn't be much help.

Well, as we read the advertisement, it was clear that those luxurious accommodations wouldn't solve any problems for us if our health failed (never mind the fact that at the time we were seeking a solution, the place hadn't even been built yet), so there we were, still in the same old quandary: What would we do?

Occasionally, over dinner, we discussed with friends the possibility of selling our homes and buying a large house big enough for all of us. We would collectively hire plenty of help, we dreamed, to shop, cook, clean, do laundry, and care for us, and we would have a jolly old time. This always seemed like a grand idea while we were enjoying good food and imbibing a generous amount of wine. The problem was, in the clear light of day, we realized that even though we loved our friends, we weren't sure we could live with them. In addition, the logistics seemed daunting—we would need an enormous house with plenty of bathrooms plus room for all that indispensable help. And what about that help? Where would we find those wonderful cooks, cleaners, caretakers, and gardeners, looking for jobs in a houseful of not-so-zippy (at best) old people? The social aspects of our plan were even dicier than the real-estate and employee aspects. What would happen if some of the people in our group ran out of money and couldn't pay their share? If they became demented and difficult? Didn't observe the house rules? Became a burden to the others? How would we deal with petty jealousies, bids for power and control, food preferences, and even everyday idiosyncrasies? Another "solution" that wouldn't solve our dilemma bit the dust.

It was at about this time that we began to notice a growing number of advertisements for assisted-living facilities. Most of them, at least in the New York area, appeared to be owned and operated by major hotel chains. We investigated and learned that, not surprisingly, these facilities are patterned pretty much in the hotel tradition. They generally offer one-room or suite accommodations and three meals a day in a restaurant-like dining room. And they are expensive; the average in New York was $3,850 a month and as much as $6,000 a month. Now, all these years later, assisted-living facilities have sprung up everywhere, some less expensive than the hotel-operated ones— but there is also an inflation factor. Here, in the suburban area of Philadelphia, the going rate for assisted living is between $4,000 and $5,000 a month. All the facilities have staff to see that medications are taken on schedule and to provide assistance with the activities of daily living—limited help with dressing, bathing, meals, and the like. Most assisted-living residences offer some social and recreational opportunities; the best of them may even have a recreation director. Since regulation of these facilities varies from state to state, the advertised assistance may or may not be adequate. The really big downside of assisted-living establishments is that they don't offer any skilled nursing. If you get seriously sick, too sick to live on your own with minimal assistance, you are back to square one: You need to make other arrangements.

In any case, at the time of discussion, we weren't candidates for assisted living. We didn't need any help and certainly weren't about to dramatically change our lifestyle to living in a hotel room! So that was out, too. Considering the limited options, we wondered if we should just chance it and grow old together in our house.

Conventional wisdom tells us that staying in our own home, if possible, is the best answer to old age. However, as every homeowner knows, houses need constant attention. The myriad chores we take in stride when we are young become onerous later on. Pruning bushes, cleaning gutters, mowing the lawn, weeding the garden, shoveling snow, and coping with hurricanes and other storms can become overwhelming and impossible. Even when there is personal nursing care at home, all those property-related chores still need to be done, and without access to a good handyman (and a fat checkbook), problems abound.

This was something we thought about and, of course, we had already seen what happened when our very ill friends became too much for a home healthcare team to handle. For confirmation, new evidence that this wasn't the way to go kept cropping up every few months. Chilling statistics informed us that over one-half of elderly women and one-third of elderly men will enter a nursing home before they die. We saw how and why it happens firsthand. Here are some examples:

Our friend Francis began to have memory problems that seemed harmless at first—difficulty remembering names and telephone numbers, misplacing his glasses and keys, or forgetting what he needed from the hardware store. But it wasn't long before his condition grew worse. He'd tell the same stories many times during the course of an evening, could not remember how long he and and his wife, Annette, had been married, or what year he had graduated from college.

When Francis got lost on his way home from the neighborhood gas station, Annette finally insisted on a medical examination. After a thor-

ough psychiatric and neurological workup at the local hospital, Francis was diagnosed with Alzheimer's disease.

Over a period of several years, Francis's condition worsened. In time, he failed to recognize friends and eventually even forgot his daughter's name. By then, he couldn't tell night from day and regularly slipped out of the house when his wife was asleep and simply wandered off "to go to the office" or "to do an errand." Whenever Annette discovered that he was missing, she'd call the village police, who soon became accustomed to hunting him down.

Annette loved Francis and wanted to take good care of him, but she often resented the fact that she had become a full-time custodian. She could no longer do anything by or for herself and most of their friends seemed to have gotten "too busy" to come by or invite them to their homes. Annette began to feel that her life was over, and she reached a point where she could barely function. She could hardly take care of herself, let alone Francis, so suddenly a nursing home became the only option.

*   *   *

Our friend Alfred, a sculptor, was a large, gregarious man who developed Parkinson's disease. For a long time he did well on medication and life continued in normal fashion for him and his wife, Betsy. They were very social and continued to give and go to parties, and Alfred continued to work. But in time, severe hand tremors forced him to give up sculpting. He grew angry and depressed, had difficulty walking, and became somewhat demented. When the dementia got worse, the couple's social life came to an end. It was all much too much for Betsy to deal with.

Fortunately, money was not a problem for this couple, so they were able to hire three shifts of nurses per day. But then Alfred became incontinent and tried to fight off the nurses when they wanted to change his clothes or his bed linens. He was tall, big-boned, and heavy, and even male nurses couldn't handle him. When two of them hurt their backs in the struggle and quit, the agency refused to send anyone else. Betsy had no choice but to send Alfred to a nursing home.

*   *   *

Cynthia, a retired teacher, became depressed when her husband of fifty-two years died. Although she was given medication for the depression, *she hardly ate, couldn't sleep, and seemed to be getting worse instead of better. Her daughter, who had a husband and two children, realized that her mother couldn't be left alone, and so the young family invited her to live with them. Cynthia seemed glad to be there, but she was still depressed and listless and became increasingly confused. The arrangement came to an abrupt end when Cynthia threw a burning candle into the trash and nearly burned down the house, and she, too, went off to a nursing home. Her small savings account, which she had meant to be an inheritance for her grandchildren, was used up within a few months and then she went on Medicaid.*

We knew all these people, and spent a lot of time visiting the well spouses who, even if they had help, were "house prisoners" because they feared what might happen if they left for even a few hours. We felt sorry for all their distraught children, whose lives were totally disrupted when they tried to help their parents. We saw marriages break up and families become virtually penniless as they used up all their resources on health care.

Somewhat to my surprise, I also discovered that home care wasn't always a good solution even for people who were only minimally physically challenged:

A widowed friend, Lucille, had a stroke but made a fairly good recovery. Her mind was sharp but her vision was poor, she was a little unsteady on her feet, and her right arm and hand were weak. It was hard for her to get around on foot, and she couldn't see well enough to read, write, or drive, so she hired a companion. She liked the companion but found her constant presence an irritant. Lucille had been an active career woman with a busy social life, but as an invalid at home she suffered from loneliness and boredom. The companion drove her to the bank, the post office, and the market, and friends came to visit from time to time, but that wasn't enough; Lucille became steadily more depressed. She did little other than watch television day and night. Without the mental stimulation she was used to and needed, she slid steadily downhill.

Morton and I also knew a number of perfectly healthy widows—

healthy but unhappy. They wandered around in houses that were too big, tried to cope with all the repairs and gardening chores that their husbands had always been in charge of, and were, without exception, lonely. The widowers seemed even worse off. Their wives had been the homemakers and social directors, and the bereaved men seemed especially sad, living in dusty houses, wearing frayed sweaters, and cooking terrible meals.

So after discovering that all the routes our friends had taken were poor ones, what were we to do? Was there a better answer? Well, it turned out that there was, and we found it. But it took a long, long time from first glimmer to *Eureka!* The next chapter tells how it happened.

CHAPTER 2

Continuing-Care Retirement Communities

Although the idea of living in a CCRC didn't immediately leap to mind, I had actually first heard about the concept a long time ago. The information came in connection with an earlier major lifestyle modification that involved a career change rather than a change of residence. After a number of years as a writer and editor, I had decided, in midlife (yes, perhaps I *was* experiencing a crisis), that I wanted to try a new career. I had long dreamed of becoming a psychotherapist and realized that, at my age, if I were going to go back to graduate school and start all over in a new field, I couldn't afford to waste any time and needed to get on with it as quickly as I could.

It was a little strange, at first, being in school with a bunch of twenty-somethings, but as they say, if you get a lemon, you might as well make lemonade. So when I learned that by taking a certain number of special courses I could become qualified as a gerontologist (one whose expertise is in the field of aging and age-related problems) as well as a mental-health counselor, I thought, "Perfect! Perhaps my graying hair will yield a payoff and I can turn all those years I've rolled up into an advantage instead of a deficit; I'll get my degree in a discipline not suitable for the very young. After all, who would have confidence in a twenty-four-year-old gerontologist?"

Now, it turns out, not surprisingly, that long-term care for the elderly was not only a recurring theme in my gerontology courses, it would be fair to say that it was *the* major theme, one that was positively harped on. The projected boom in the elderly population and the resulting increase in dementias and other age-related disorders were the meat and potatoes of many of my courses. What to do about long-term care was the end point of every discussion.

I learned a great deal about nursing homes, assisted living, and home care, but very little about the then relatively new concept of CCRCs. These, I was told, provided continuing levels of care, from none at all for the healthy (independent living), to assisted living, to skilled nursing (nursing home), to hospice care, and right on through to the end of life. All these levels, situated on a single campus, would make for smooth transitions as needs changed and would cause minimum disruption to elderly people and their families alike.

It seemed like an interesting concept, but it was all a little vague in my mind. I went on field trips to nursing homes and did an internship in a day-care center for the elderly, but I'd never visited a CCRC. As a result, although I understood the concept perfectly well, I had no picture at all of how the concept would work in real life. However, the idea was intriguing enough that I filed it in my mental good-stuff-to-remember slot for possible use in some distant future.

As it turned out, after I got my graduate degree, I was lucky enough to get a job in a general mental-health clinic. I simultaneously started a private psychotherapy practice, which flourished after the usual slow start. But since the bulk of my clients in both settings were relatively young, I never got to do much hands-on work in gerontology. Immersed in other issues, I eventually stopped keeping up with all the developments in the aging field.

But, of course, as the elderly population had continued to burgeon, so had the developments. There were many, and one that had come to the forefront was that the idea of continuing care had not only taken root, but had taken off. Started by the Society of Friends in the Philadelphia area, such communities were sprouting like mushrooms there and elsewhere. By the time I began looking for the best plan for our own late years and remembered what had seemed like such a good—but vague—idea back in school, I was surprised to find that CCRCs had become big business. Although there were a few quietly scattered around as early as the 1960s, they had suddenly proliferated during the 1980s, and by the mid-1990s, they seemed to be popping up all over the map.

Now there are CCRCs nearly everywhere, with large numbers of them in some states, relatively few in others. At the time my own search began, my home state of New York had no CCRCs at all. No wonder I hadn't been aware of their growing popularity; no one in my part of the country knew or talked about them. It turned out that because of some earlier nursing-home scandals, New York had passed laws prohibiting advance payment for future health care. CCRCs, which function by charging an entry fee that covers long-term care if and when it's needed, fell afoul of the regulations.

That law was changed a few years later. A number of CCRCs have opened in the state and many more have been planned and are being built. Throughout the nation, there are now 2,200 in operation with 628,000 living units, and those numbers continue to grow rapidly. Roughly 13 percent of the residents (but one-third of those living independently in their own apartments or villas) are married couples. Overall, about three-quarters of the residents are female and one-quarter are male.

With so many CCRCs scattered around who knew where and no idea how to get reliable information about them, I was trying hard to figure out how they worked, what they offered, and what they cost, and attempting to understand the differences among them; it was a daunting task. A couple of things quickly became very clear: I had a lot to learn, and I couldn't learn much of what I most needed to know from the seductive and beautifully produced glossy brochures that all the CCRCs were eager to send us.

After a staggering amount of tedious research, trial, error, near misses, travel, expense, and a great deal of good luck, Morton and I eventually made our way to a happy landing in the CCRC I'll call Kimberly Hills (not its real name). The rest of this book is an account of how we searched, what we learned, how and why we made the choice, and what it was like to move to—and live in—a CCRC. It is my hope that this report on our experience will spare you much of the bewilderment, labor, and risk we underwent (we came within a whisker of making a very serious mistake).

But first, let me explain exactly what CCRCs are. Since they vary very widely in type, quality, appearance, cost, population, philosophy, and amenities, I will stick to a generic description here. All the many details will follow later.

UNDERSTANDING WHAT CCRCs ARE ALL ABOUT

Basically, a CCRC is a retirement community—run either for profit or not for profit—where healthy people usually sixty years old or older can continue their accustomed lifestyle without the cares and problems of home ownership. Applicants must be in good enough health to be able to live independently and safely. (Health records confirming this are generally requested prior to admission.) Chronic conditions such as arthritis, hypertension, and osteoporosis, which are common after midlife, should not hinder acceptance, but any condition requiring nursing care probably will. Some CCRCs will admit people who are impaired by strokes, cancer, or other serious illnesses, but they will not be covered under the health contract for those ailments and will have to pay for any services they receive.

Residents can choose to live in a house (villa or cottage), a garden apartment, a high-rise apartment, or a condo-like apartment in a two- or three-story building. There are typically several hundred residents on campus, sometimes more or fewer. Residents generally have a car (or cars), and they come and go as they always have, pursue their own interests, socialize with old friends if they are from the area, and even continue to go to work each day.

The CCRC staff maintains the premises, cuts the grass, tends the pool, and plows the snow—in other words, the staff attends to all the nitty-gritty details of life. Residents may be entitled to one to three meals a day served in a dining room, but they can usually pay for additional meals or choose a no-meal plan and do their own cooking. Weekly housekeeping is provided and, almost always, sheets and towels are laundered as well. Sports facilities, entertainment, special events, and amenities abound.

By far the most common arrangement is for residents to pay an entry fee when they move in and a monthly fee thereafter. The entry fee is almost always refundable for a short period of time in case the resident feels he or she has made a mistake and decides to move. And it is usually refundable later, as well, or to the estate when the residents die. Many CCRCs offer entry-fee refunds of 100 percent upon the death o the resident, and some CCRCs offer more than one plan, such as a

50-percent refund. Generally, the smaller the refund, the lower the monthly fee.

There are some CCRCs that offer rental arrangements without an entry fee. These are especially attractive to those who can pay a monthly fee but who are unable or unwilling to make a big payment up front. However, the monthly fees are generally higher when there is no entry fee.

A few CCRCs are co-ops or condos in which a living unit is actually purchased. This concept probably originated so that homeowners could save on capital gains tax by rolling over the profit when they sold their homes. But since the changes in the tax laws, there is a large enough tax-free allowance on the sale of a home to make it unnecessary for all but a very few to purchase real estate in order to avoid tax. However, some people who have always been owners are set on the idea of owning their home. If you are among them, keep in mind that you will really *own* it, with all that implies. You will be responsible for interior repairs and upkeep, such as painting. (In a non-owned CCRC unit, if a pipe breaks or if your toilet overflows, you call service and it's attended to. No problem.) Keep in mind, too, that if you or your estate wants to sell a CCRC co-op or condo, the buyer must meet the entrance requirements of the CCRC. And, of course, as in any real-estate sale, a profit or a loss might result. If a newer, flashier CCRC has gone up nearby, there will probably be a loss. It the unit has appreciated in value, the contract may, or may not, call for the CCRC to be a partner in the profit.

Entry fees and monthly fees vary widely. They depend on the kind of residence occupied, the type of healthcare contract chosen, the geographical location and its land values, the financial structure of the CCRC, the amenities offered, and the payment plan. Among the least expensive CCRCs are those sponsored by religious organizations, some of which require no entry fee at all. At the time of this writing, the average entry fee is about $110,000, but can range from about $25,000 to $300,000 with a very rare high of over $500,000 (for a large and luxurious house in an expensive area); monthly fees can range from about $200 to $4,000 with an additional charge for a second person. An average monthly fee for a studio apartment is $1,080 and $1,620 for a two-bedroom apartment. Those who have been homeowners can generally meet the entry fee from the proceeds of their house sale. (Precise charges can be obtained by calling the marketing department at CCRCs of interest.)

If the monthly fees for the kind of accommodation you want seem high at first glance, consider that they generally include health care (depending on the contract), at least one meal a day, housekeeping, cable television, electricity, hot water, heating and air conditioning, all grounds and building maintenance, sports and exercise facilities, entertainment, and scores of amenities. After adding up their costs, many homeowners find that the monthly fee is comparable to what they're used to spending—and it may even be less. And that's *not* including the priceless advantage of security and peace of mind.

Record your monthly household expenses and the projected fees for the CCRC in Table 2.1 below. Chances are you will find that CCRC living fits into your budget.

TABLE 2.1 MONTHLY COST COMPARISON		
	HOUSEHOLD EXPENSES	CCRC FEES
MAJOR EXPENSES		
Homeowner's insurance or renter's insurance		
Mortgage/rent or monthly fee		
Real estate taxes		NA
Health insurance (Medicare and MediGap)/ Long-term-care insurance		
MISCELLANEOUS EXPENSES		
Cable television		
Electricity		NA
Exterior painting		NA
Food		NA
Fitness-center membership		NA

	HOUSEHOLD EXPENSES	**CCRC FEES**
MISCELLANEOUS EXPENSES (cont.)		
Grounds care		NA
Heating and air conditioning		NA
Housekeeping		NA
Interior painting		NA
Internet service		
Pool service		NA
Repairs, maintenance, and/or replacement of appliances, roof, plumbing, wiring, etc.		NA
Security system		NA
Service policies		NA
Snow plowing		NA
Telephone		
Tips to service workers or suggested cash gifts		
Trash removal		NA
Trips to medical appointments		
Water charges		NA
Window washing		NA
Other		
SUBTOTAL		
ALLOWABLE TAX DEDUCTIONS (if applicable)		
Home mortgage interest		
Medical expense deduction		
Other		
TOTAL		

All CCRCs provide for health care on the premises when illness or disability strikes, and this is what CCRCs are all about in the first place. There are various kinds of plans; each is spelled out in the facility's contract or agreement. Although people have reasons (including a certain amount of denial about their future healthcare needs) for choosing plans that are not all-inclusive, my own very strong bias is for an extensive agreement that guarantees you whatever care you need for the rest of your life. This includes assisted living or short-term or long-term nursing care with no extra charge (except, perhaps, some small incidentals) for as long as you need it. No surprises, no hassles, no long wait to get into a nursing home. When we were shopping for a CCRC, we did not visit or even consider any place that did not offer an extensive agreement. (See "Types of CCRC Contracts" on page 21.)

Whether you are healthy or not, a good CCRC offers a supportive environment with broad opportunities for enjoyment, growth, friendship, and recreational and cultural activities. And even for the healthiest, nursing care is often needed on a temporary basis. For example, following a fracture or surgery, an elective procedure, or any illness or injury requiring hospitalization, the patient is discharged as soon as possible to recuperate among friends and with excellent (one certainly hopes!) care back at the CCRC.

Should long-term nursing care become necessary for a resident, he or she can make the transition without the shock of a move to a strange place away from friends. And if there is a spouse, what a comfort it is to be right there, on the campus, able to visit many times a day or night without having to travel.

The following is a summary of the many advantages of CCRC living:

- In a good CCRC, access to health care is unlimited. There is onsite care for routine checkups, emergency response around the clock, and, if major illness strikes, skilled nursing for as long as it is needed without extra charge (assuming an extensive contract exists).

- Residents have security, both physical and financial (allowing for rising costs). The environment is a safe and comfortable one, and assistance is always available. There are no concerns about intruders, muggings, or robbery. In case of injury or sudden illness, there are alarm cords or telephones in every room to bring immediate help.

TYPES OF CCRC CONTRACTS

A contract is a legal business agreement that details what goods and services the CCRC will provide and what your obligations as a resident will be. In general, there are three types of contracts from which to choose. Each type is discussed below. Keep in mind, however, that although their broad concepts are the same, no two CCRCs will offer identical agreements. Therefore, no matter which type of contract you choose, you must read every word of the fine print and always have your lawyer review it.

Extensive, or All-Inclusive, Agreement

An extensive, or all-inclusive, agreement is the only contract that won't surprise you with big medical bills if you get sick. It includes all your living costs *plus* as much assisted living or nursing care as you need at no additional cost (except for incidentals such as extra meals or special supplies). The entry fee and/or monthly fee will be higher than they are with other types of contracts, but the extra dollars are like insurance premiums that pay for unlimited health care if required.

Modified Agreement

A modified agreement, in addition to your normal living costs, usually allows you a specified number of days of assisted living or nursing care after which you have to pay a per-diem fee, the amount of which will vary from community to community. There are very wide variations in such policies; they may include as few as thirty days or as many as several months in the nursing center.

Fee-for-Service Agreement

A fee-for-service agreement offers the lowest entry and monthly fees. It provides normal residential services, but it makes no provision for assisted living or nursing care. As the name of this type of contract suggests, it calls for a fee to be paid when services are received.

This may be a feasible arrangement for you if you already have long-term-care insurance at a reasonable premium. But make sure that you are perfectly clear on how the insurance will affect your charges at the CCRC if you choose this type of contract.

- Assuming the CCRC is financially secure (more on this later), a non-profit CCRC generally guarantees care for life even if a resident outlives his or her funds. Although our financial advisors may tell us that our nest egg is adequate to see us through, most of us worry (especially we of the Great Depression generation) about inflation, recessions, depressions, and maybe just plain bad luck. Knowing that you won't be put out on the street can be a big comfort.

- Harder to quantify, but just as important as health care and financial security, is the tremendous psychological and emotional support a CCRC offers. With that special cohesiveness that groups of all like-minded people develop, the community becomes a caring, compassionate, extended family. If you move in as a married couple, and later, your spouse dies, you will grieve to be sure. But losing a spouse in a close, supportive community is a totally different experience from sustaining such a loss and being alone in your own home. A CCRC has many people who have been through it and know what it's like. With heartfelt empathy and sympathy, they will reach out to include you in everything from sharing a dining table to being a partner at bridge. For professional help, there is bound to be a mental-health counselor on the staff, usually one or more psychiatrists, and, in all likelihood, a bereavement support group.

- At all times there is a powerful *esprit de corps*—a strong sense of "We're in this together, we have similar concerns, and it helps us all if we pull together and help each other out." Numerous studies have proven the importance of peer relationships to elderly people. Such relationships are generally even more important to their sense of well-being than their relationships with relatives. A CCRC provides unlimited opportunities for friendship and socializing. When people lose some of their physical mobility or their ability to drive, they may have few ways to get together with others in an outside community, but in a CCRC, meeting friends is always easy.

    Perhaps surprisingly (but only to young people), a number of romances develop in CCRCs between widows and widowers who were sure they would never love again. We are never too old to value and desire affection and companionship.

MEET ELSIE, A TYPICAL CCRC RESIDENT

Elsie Clifton is a typical CCRC resident. She was the wife of a businessman, the mother of three, and a hard worker in her church and for several charities. She had married young and helped to put her husband, George, through college while he worked part time. Although she had hoped to get a college degree herself after George graduated, it didn't work out as planned. By the time George was earning an adequate living, World War II was raging and Elsie was pregnant.

After the children were grown and out of the house, the Cliftons began to travel frequently. They went to Europe every year and visited their children and grandchildren in three different states. When not vacationing, George had his career and Elsie managed the house and garden and was deeply involved in her community work. On weekends they played golf and socialized with friends.

When George died, Elsie found herself feeling very alone. She was in her upper sixties and in good health, but she just wasn't enjoying life anymore. The children talked among themselves about how much their mother had changed, how the sparkle had gone out of her, and they were deeply concerned but didn't know what to do—especially since Elsie kept insisting that she was fine.

There seemed to be no solution in sight until a next-door neighbor of one of the children announced that she was moving to a CCRC. When the neighbor showed Elsie's daughter the brochure, she was impressed. She called each of her siblings, and they all agreed that it looked like a perfect idea for their mother.

Elsie couldn't bear the thought of leaving her house, her garden, her church, or her friends. She wasn't about to move into a place that might turn out to be institutional, and she wasn't about to go live with a bunch of strangers. It was out of the question, she said. Her children weren't easily discouraged, however. They did their homework, checked resources, gathered information, and discovered what sounded like a very good CCRC only a half hour away from Elsie's home. After much cajoling, one of the children finally got Elsie to visit the place.

They spent an entire day there and were so impressed with what they saw that they decided to go back the next day and look around some more. Elsie was still skeptical, but there were a few cracks in her armor. She hadn't expected such beautiful grounds, spacious apartments, or so many welcoming, friendly people who spoke to her just because they recognized her as a stranger. Elsie wouldn't admit it to the children, but it looked like a community she might be able to live in. And it would be a short drive to get back to visit her old friends and haunts. The process of change had begun and took a big leap forward when Elsie found two of her old school chums happily in residence there.

It was more than a year and three visits later before Elsie finally made up her mind—long after her children had wisely decided to back off—that a move to the CCRC might be a good idea after all. It took many months more to select the apartment she wanted, sell her house, move, and get settled into life in the community.

But settle in she did—with enthusiasm. Because she was used to being active in community work, it didn't take Elsie long to find her niche on several committees. She's back to playing weekend golf with three new friends, has joined the ceramics workshop and found that she has a real gift for throwing pots, and best of all, she is enrolled in two courses at the local college for the fall semester.

- Opportunities for volunteerism and participation on committees or in groups are easily available to everyone in a CCRC. Older people who live at home may no longer want to drive at night—or at all— or find it difficult for other reasons to get around to the meetings, religious services, and functions they used to frequent. In a CCRC, it's easy to attend the many in-house events or take advantage of the provided bus service to selected trips off campus.

- The opportunity for lifetime learning is easy, too, at CCRCs. Recent studies have shown that those who keep their minds active are far less prone to develop Alzheimer's disease or other dementias than those who stagnate. One of our criteria in choosing a CCRC was to be near one or more universities so that we could take advantage of the opportunities many of them offer seniors to audit courses for little or no fee. But there is also ample opportunity for learning without ever leaving the campus. There are generally lectures by learned experts and, often, structured classes of one sort or another. For example, at many CCRCs, large numbers of residents who had never before been within touching distance of a computer have learned, with the help of free instruction and computer access, to communicate with their friends and families through e-mail, and to explore the wonders of the Internet. Even the least technically adventurous have learned to play solitaire and FreeCell with panache, and many have gone on to get their own computers.

A FEW DISADVANTAGES OF CCRC LIVING

After devoting so much space to the advantages of CCRCs, I must admit to a few caveats. So here they are: The first three are *cost, cost,* and *cost.* Although there is a wide range in fees, CCRCs are not for those with little, or no, money. A few CCRCs, usually those that are church sponsored, may offer "scholarships" or other financial aid, particularly for members of the church. But by and large, since CCRCs tend to be at least somewhat upscale, they are planned for the middle-class market and usually require an outlay of capital, especially for an extensive contract. Obviously, the more upscale the place you choose and the better the contract, the pricier it will be. While a fee-for-service contract (residents pay for health care as needed) makes for low cost, it also eliminates the security that is one of the CCRCs' chief advantages— unless, of course, you already have long-term-care insurance in place. If you do, you will have to talk it over with the CCRC, get all the figures, and work through the arithmetic to see what plan is best for you. (See "Financial Formulas for Acceptance" on page 26 for more on financial considerations.)

Rich or poor, there are probably only very few people who are not suited to the CCRC lifestyle. These include people who feel uncomfortable in social situations and generally consider themselves loners. Also, as in any small community, every CCRC has certain norms that must be observed. Someone who hangs around in robe and slippers all day and evening would be irked by the dining-room dress codes, and one who never dines before 10 PM would find the dining-room hours impossible.

FINANCIAL FORMULAS
FOR ACCEPTANCE

CCRCs generally require a current financial statement from you before accepting you. The formulas for acceptance vary, but as a rule of thumb, they want you to have a monthly income that is about one and a half to two times your monthly fee. The income may come from social security, IRAs, interest, pensions, investments, annuities, or any other source. Here are two examples of acceptable financial situations:

Mrs. Z is a widow who wants a one-bedroom apartment in a CCRC in California and an extensive agreement. The entry fee is $85,000 and the monthly fee is $1,300. She will need to have an annual income of between $23,400 and $31,200. She can sell the house she and her late husband built forty years ago for $240,000. After she pays her entry fee she will have $155,000 left. Her banker tells her that if he conservatively and safely invests that sum she can get a yield of 4 percent, or $6,200. She gets $1,100 a month—$13,200 a year—from her husband's social security, $15,000 from savings the couple had put into an annuity, and about $4,000 in interest and dividends from a small portfolio of stocks and bonds. She has an income of $38,400 a year, much more than she needs to qualify.

There may be rules about cleaning up after your pets, parking, recycling, or late-night noise that would be annoying to someone who is used to doing whatever he or she likes.

And lastly, a CCRC on a shaky financial footing could be a major disaster for anyone who committed to it with the payment of a large entry fee. There were financial problems and a rash of bankruptcies some years ago when the industry was new, but today most CCRCs are in good financial shape and about three-quarters of the states have strong regulatory laws to make sure they stay that way. Moreover, there are ways to protect yourself from putting your money into a CCRC that could go bankrupt sometime down the road. One way is to choose a CCRC that is accredited by the Continuing Care Accreditation Commission (CCAC), an independent body whose many criteria include

* * *

Mr. and Mrs. R have paid for long-term-care insurance for more than ten years. Recently, Mr. R had a stroke and is seriously disabled. Mrs. R tried to care for him at home with some part-time nursing help, but it didn't work out. She has taken a two-bedroom apartment at a CCRC in Massachusetts where Mr. R cannot be accepted as a resident since he isn't capable of living independently. He went directly into the CCRC's nursing unit and the fees for his care are paid by his long-term-care insurance. Mrs. R is the sole resident of the apartment. The entry fee was $250,223 and the monthly fee is $1,240 or $14,880 a year. The required income of between $22,320 and $29,760 is no problem since, until his stroke, Mr. R was a partner in a prestigious law firm; he has a sizable pension and savings. The doctors are encouraged by the progress Mr. R is making with the help of the physical therapy he is receiving, and they are hopeful that he will soon be mobile again.

If that happens, and he is well enough to live on his own, he will move into the apartment with his wife. At that time Mr. and Mrs. R will have to pay an additional $10,000 for a second-person entry fee and $880 more per month for two-person occupancy, which is no problem for this financially secure couple. From that point on, Mr. R will be a full-fledged resident and will be entitled to the same care and amenities as his wife.

financial stability. The role of the CCAC will be explained in more detail in the next chapter.

It is my own, admittedly, very biased judgment that the advantages strongly outweigh the disadvantages—unless, of course, you're one of those all-day-in-pajamas, late-night noise makers. And even if you are, review what your alternatives to a CCRC might be if you should become too disabled to be on your own. You can also hope—and gamble—that you will never become disabled, and you may be lucky.

And since you must be capable of independent living when you enter a CCRC, if you wait until you *need* care, you have waited too long. So in the interest of independence and self-direction, as well as getting accepted in the first place, you have to choose a CCRC while you are still healthy and can call all the shots.

CHAPTER 3

The Search for a "Perfect" Community

Perhaps your interest has been piqued and you've concluded that a CCRC might be a good idea for you—if you can find the right one. How do you go about getting the information you need? There's so much of it available that you have to be systematic in your approach. So, before you go to the trouble of collecting a lot of data you don't want, first make a rough assessment of what you *do* want.

If you are starting from scratch, you will want to use the excellent directories of CCRCs available on the Internet (see the Resources section). Since CCRC listings are generally arranged by state and city, researching a particular location is a handy way to start your search. The directories also provide information on the kinds of contracts various CCRCs offer, the size and type of communities, their location and settings, types of living units, fees and charges, meal plans, and amenities. There's a lot of information to take in, but if you know what your needs are, you can narrow your search considerably.

LOCATION

Everyone has personal criteria for location, and the most common ones are to stay close to children or to move to a more pleasing climate. City people often want to remain in an urban area, and country people generally seek peace, quiet, space, and trees. When Morton and I started our search, we had certain location criteria: We wanted to be no more than two hours from New York City because most of our children and grandchildren were there. Since there were no CCRCs near our home, we lacked the option of staying in the neighborhood, and since most of our friends were in New York, they fell under the same two-hour rule as our family. That immediately narrowed our search to three states: Connecticut, New Jersey, and Pennsylvania.

A second criterion for location was our preference for a country setting, either truly rural or woodsy-suburban, but close enough to a city so that we could easily get to urban cultural events, good libraries, and universities. We also wanted the urban advantage of an excellent hospital and medical services.

NON-PROFIT VERSUS FOR-PROFIT STATUS

An eventual major consideration for us would be to live in a CCRC that was non-profit; unfortunately, that bit of wisdom didn't come to us until we had already been looking for a year. "Freshly Squeezed at Holly Grove" on page 31 tells you how we got our education on that point (and wasted time until we did).

After our experiences with Holly Grove, non-profit status became an essential feature for us. The differences, both philosophical and financial, are enormous. If you have money to spare and no concerns about spending or outliving it, and the CCRC in your neighborhood happens to be for-profit and you like its looks and what you've heard about it, check it out—but do be just a little bit more careful.

Having begun to learn how much CCRCs differ from one another in myriad ways and that you can't necessarily judge them by looking, we went a step further in refining our search. First, we discovered that most non-profit CCRCs are members of the American Association of Homes and Services for the Aging (AAHSA), a body that represents 5,600 non-profit organizations providing health care, housing, and services to the elderly. Their print directory of CCRCs (which is, unfortunately, no longer published) became our major source of information since there was not yet, at that time, anything much to be found on the Internet. We obtained a wealth of invaluable data from AAHSA, not the least of which concerned accreditation; we had never even heard of it when we began our quest.

FRESHLY SQUEEZED AT HOLLY GROVE

On the recommendation of a friend, we went to visit Holly Grove (another fictitious name) in Connecticut. It was pretty, we loved the fact that it was close to Yale and to the beach, and the marketing department put us up in grand style in a lovely apartment. We met some great people, had an excellent dinner, and were quite taken with the place. So much so, that at the urging of the marketing director, we left behind a "refundable" check for $2,000 to reserve a place on the waiting list.

It was only after we eventually got hold of the agreement that we noticed a few major differences from the two non-profit CCRCs we had visited earlier. Unlike them, Holly Grove did not guarantee to keep us for life if we ran out of money; private rooms in the nursing facility cost extra; prescription drugs were not included in the monthly fees; and we would have to pay imputed tax (more on this later) to the IRS. On a petty level, we were bowled over to discover that while weekly housekeeping was included in the tariff, there was an extra charge for having the housekeeper change the bed linens.

By then we had begun to realize that for-profit CCRCs are what they sound like: for profit. But we were still in for a surprise. We wrote to Holly Grove asking for the return of our refundable deposit and were stunned to receive a check for $1,000 instead of the $2,000 we had paid. A reply to our letter of inquiry assured us that we had been handed some document or other that had clearly spelled out Holly Grove's policy of keeping $1,000 to cover "administrative costs" and, sure enough, just as they said, we found the information, in very small type, buried somewhere in a sea of words. It was our own fault, to be sure. We had assumed that all CCRCs held back the same small amount to cover paper work and postage, and, moreover, that they were all as benign as they looked. Lesson learned: we needed to be less naïve and more vigilant.

ACCREDITATION

We all know about academic accreditation. When your child goes off to college, you want to be certain that the chosen institution is accredited so that you can depend on its conforming to certain standards. Accreditation for a CCRC is a similar credential, and it gives you the same kind of assurance. The accrediting agency is the Continuing Care Accreditation Commission (CCAC), an independent body sponsored by the AAHSA. Their standards are extremely high and cover such areas as resident life, health, and wellness; financial resources and disclosure; and governance and administration. If you look over the following summary of the standards, you will see that they provide reassuring safeguards in those vital but tricky areas that you would have great trouble researching on your own—particularly those relating to the financial structure and soundness of the organization. The following, in abbreviated form, are the CCAC's Standards of Excellence—their requirements for accreditation.

Resident Life, Health, and Wellness

- The well-being of the organization is sustained through involvement of residents in responsible and constructive self-governance and activities planning.

- The organization's physical environment is well maintained and attractive, and fully addresses access, health, safety, and other applicable law or regulatory requirements at all levels of care.

- Health and wellness programs are provided by staff who have the appropriate training, knowledge, and experience to meet the needs of residents.

- The governing board ensures that ethical principles are followed in fulfilling the organization's mission.

Financial Resources and Disclosure

- The organization has a clearly defined budget process by which the budget is established and monitored.

- The organization establishes and maintains adequate cash and investments or other financial assets for long-term financial viability.

- The organization has appropriate management information and assistance to utilize and provide a basis for determining, monitoring, analyzing, and controlling its financial operations.

- The organization discloses to residents, sponsors, and other appropriate parties information that explains its assets and liabilities; reflects the position of any parent organizations; and discloses any material relationships with other entities.

Governance and Administration

- The governing board appoints a chief executive officer/president or executive director/administrator who is accountable to the board, and conducts an annual review of the CEO's performance.

- The organization has an integrated strategic and financial-planning process.

- Open communication channels exist throughout all levels of the organization.

- Prospective residents receive the organization's mission statement, resident agreement, financial disclosure, schedules of current fees, charges for all services, refund policy (if applicable), and other essential information prior to moving in.

That last item brings to mind another grievance against the infamous Holly Grove: While we were still on their waiting list, they raised the entry fee by $10,000 but never bothered to notify us! Had we decided to move there, we might not have found out about the increase until we were packed to go.

Becoming accredited is a completely voluntary procedure, and it requires an enormous amount of work on the part of the CCRC staff. They must prepare a large number of detailed documents, keep meticulous records, periodically submit audited financial statements, adhere scrupulously to the highest standards, and accede to numerous onsite inspections. The entire procedure must be repeated every five years, so that once accreditation has been granted, it's almost time to start preparing for the next round. Some CCRCs are willing to forgo accreditation rather than go through all that, and some are too new to quali-fy because they don't yet have a long enough track record. That lack of a track record, by the way, is a good reason to be wary of start-up CCRCs. Typically, future residents are solicited before the ground has even been broken. We felt—and still do—that committing to an entity that doesn't yet exist is a risky business, not to mention the probable inconveniences of embarking on a shakedown cruise.

In addition to the CCRCs that do not want the bother of preparing for accreditation, many simply cannot meet the rigorous requirements. But there are now 338 CCAC-accredited CCRCs (with more to be added in the near future) in thirty-one states and the District of Colum-bia; as interest and knowledge on the part of consumers and competi-tion among marketers continue to grow, the number of accredited CCRCs is sure to proliferate.

After we found out about accreditation and realized what a safety net it was for those aspects of operation that were invisible to us, we added it to our list of criteria. That doesn't mean that you have to do likewise. There are undoubtedly some perfectly fine CCRCs that are not accredited. If you are strongly drawn to one of them, you can make a pretty sound assessment on your own by noting all the guidelines set forth in the rest of this book. Get help from your attorney and a certified public accountant, preferably one who has experience with CCRCs, in assessing the financial stability of the organization. Contact the Better Business Bureau and your state's Department of Insurance (often a governing body for CCRCs) for additional information. We checked all sources but remained very cautious and just felt safest with the CCAC seal of approval, so decided we wouldn't do without it.

HEALTH CARE

The matter we were most cautious about was health care. After all, we weren't thinking about moving to a CCRC because we love to move. It was those first two letters, the *CC* for *continuing care,* that were para-mount. We were interested only in CCRCs that offered an extensive contract, which would guarantee long-term health care. We weren't able to learn much else about the healthcare offerings until we actually made visits, but choosing only places that offered extensive contracts was a starting point. Later, some of our most urgent questions would be: Are there doctors on the premises daily? How much assistance is given in assisted living? What are the living quarters like? Does the nursing home have private rooms? How many patients are there per nurse? If I require care for an extended time, will I be able to return to my own home when I'm well?

SUMMING UP THE SEARCH

We started our search for a CCRC by using the now-out-of-print AAHSA Directory. We went through the listings for our three chosen states, map in hand, keeping in mind our two-hour travel limit from New York City. After checking off the CCRCs in our geographical ballpark, we excluded all those that didn't fit our other criteria. We tried to be very systematic in order to save time, energy, money, and running to and fro to look at CCRCs that weren't right for us, but we were inefficient anyway because there was too much we didn't know to get it right at first.

To help you avoid some of the blunders we made, here are some important steps for you to follow:

1. Using one or more of the CCRC Internet directories, select your geographical area based on proximity to home, family, work, good climate, and so on.

2. If you have a clear preference, screen for a rural, suburban, or urban setting.

3. Rule out any places that do not offer the kind of living unit you desire.

4. Decide whether you want only a non-profit CCRC (recommended).

5. Decide if you want a CCRC that is accredited by the Continuing Care Accreditation Commission (recommended).

6. Decide if you want only an extensive contract (recommended), a modified contract, or a fee-for-service contract.

7. Of the CCRCs that remain on your list, rule out any that are too expensive.

8. If there are certain amenities you cannot do without (golf, tennis, fitness program, Jacuzzi, whatever), rule out those places that lack them.

By now, you should have a good working list of CCRCs you want detailed information from. If you are using the Internet, you will find that many CCRCs have their own websites and some of those can even give you a virtual tour of the campus with all the amenities. (The website address is often the name of the CCRC and ends either in *.org* if it is non-profit or *.com* if it is for-profit.) This valuable shortcut was nonexistent when we were starting out, but by using it, you will save a lot of time and trouble and be greatly helped in refining your list of possible CCRCs.

So now, with that list on your desk, it is time to telephone, e-mail, or write to the CCRCs to ask for information packets. Then watch your mailbox, because this is where the search begins to get interesting.

CHAPTER 4

Looking Over the Information Packets

Your effort is soon rewarded by a mailbox stuffed with large envelopes containing beautifully produced, colorful brochures on heavy, expensive paper. It's easy to be seduced by the handsomest of these since it's natural to assume that the excellent taste displayed in the elegant design is a reflection of the CCRC that sent it to you. This is certainly true to some extent because someone at the CCRC was instrumental in planning, approving, and paying for the material. But do keep in mind that the brochure was created by an advertising agency hired to pique your interest and make you feel that you need look no further for you have just found the home of your dreams. It is important to remember, too, that CCRCs are a highly competitive business and a savvy marketing department will spare no expense to have this essential marketing tool well produced.

Having noted all that, you can proceed to gather quite a lot of information from the mailings. If the community is accredited, the brochure will tell you so and it will bear the seal of the CCAC. It will also, almost always, include a mission statement that sets forth the philosophy and goals of the CCRC. At a quick glance, they all look good, but if you study them carefully, you will find differences that provide important information. I personally like to see references in the mission statement to life care; to respecting the worth and dignity of every resident; to caring for the social, spiritual, and recreational well-being as well as the health of each individual; and to financial responsibility on the part of management.

The pictures are informative, too. They usually give you an idea of the style of the buildings and the appearance of the grounds, and they generally include interior pictures of dining rooms, lounges, athletic facilities, and living quarters. The pictures show you the best they have to offer, so if you find them unattractive, then that place is definitely not for you. Even pictures of residents may be telling: their clothing, hairstyles, and general demeanor may provide subtle clues about the mores of the population.

A couple of CCRCs sent us videos along with their print packages. They were interesting and revealed more than the brochures, but the same caveats apply. All the people (residents? actors?) in them looked ecstatically happy, or were exercising vigorously, or dining sumptuously. Odd, perhaps, but we were not moved to visit either of the places that sent videos. I don't know whether it was because we found the videos overly slick and commercial, too hard sell, or whether the places didn't appeal to us for other reasons, perhaps some that we weren't even conscious of.

Site plans and maps, usually part of any presentation, will help you figure out whether the location conforms to your preference for an urban, suburban, or country setting, and you can get some valuable information about the campus and its surroundings. If you're a nature and greenery lover, you will want to know the acreage of the community. How much open space is there? Are there walking trails? What kinds of plantings are there? What is the neighborhood like? Are there are points of special interest or beauty nearby? How convenient is the location for travel? How far is it from the airport? A train? If the CCRC is in a city, what is it near? What kind of public transportation is there and how convenient is it? Is the neighborhood safe? Does the CCRC have grounds and/or are there parks nearby? In any setting, what are the buildings like? High-rise? Several stories? Single story? What architectural style? Are the apartment buildings and villas attractive?

Keep in mind that if you move there, it will be your neighborhood and your home. Don't waste any time on it if you hate the way it looks or even if you're lukewarm. Learn as much as you can but know that it's possible to be fooled by artfully angled or cropped photos. We took at least two long trips to visit places that only vaguely resembled the beautiful pictures we had seen; one looked dark, gloomy, and forbidding, a little like a prison; the other was plunked down behind a parking lot in a rundown neighborhood and was almost devoid of grass, trees, flowers, charm, or grace.

LIVING ARRANGEMENTS

If you approve of the brochure, it's time to study the floor plans. Do you want an apartment or a villa/cottage? Does the CCRC offer both? How many bedrooms do you want? Floor plans usually give the total square footage of the unit in addition to room dimensions, and there are surprisingly large differences in one- or two-bedroom units from place to place. (The average area of a two-bedroom apartment is 1,000 to 1,300 square feet—with a few smaller and a few considerably larger in locales where either land is not at a premium or high prices will fly.) Are there apartments with dens? With balconies or patios? Are there plenty of windows to assure that the apartment will get enough light? Is there sufficient closet space? Enough kitchen cabinets? Don't even hope to fit the entire contents of your big house into an apartment, but there should be enough space so that you can live graciously and don't have to get rid of *all* your treasures.

If you like lots of room and can afford it, look for upscale CCRCs that offer more than a two-bedroom unit. Many of the newer ones have apartments with three bedrooms or more. The early planners of CCRCs thought that small apartments would be most in demand, but this has proven to be wrong. New communities are vying with one another for generous space, and older ones are trying to expand. Here at Kimberly Hills, the newest and largest villas have nine or ten rooms, more than 4,000 square feet on two levels (with an optional elevator!) and a two-car garage. They are elegant, have every amenity—and come at a price that is surely not for everyone. On the other hand, if *economy* is your watchword, and you are alone, perhaps you will opt for a very affordable studio apartment. Not all CCRCs offer studios, so again, save time by crossing off places that don't offer what you want.

While you can learn a great deal from floor plans, even with extraordinary visual skills, it is probably impossible to get a crystal-clear idea of what an apartment or villa looks like until you've been in it. The "feel" of a dwelling depends on the light, and the way the space flows—or doesn't—as much as on square footage. But paper assess-ments are a useful preliminary to visits.

The choice between an apartment and a villa can be tricky. Most people leaving a house prefer the idea of a villa because it represents less of a change and so makes for an easier transition. There are front and back doors, a yard and garden, often a fireplace, basement, attic, and a one- or two-car garage. It's just like home! At first, we were sure that was what we wanted. We were even particularly attracted to a CCRC that had *only* cottages—each with its own flower garden and white picket fence.

But then we started to remember why we were going to live in a CCRC in the first place. It was our plan for a future when we would surely be less healthy and able, perhaps even *dis*abled, and we began to rethink the cottage idea. In virtually every CCRC, all but one that we investigated, the apartments are connected by corridors to the central common rooms—the dining room, coffee shop, auditorium, fitness cen-ter, mail room, and so forth. That means that in bad weather you can get around under cover and, if you need to use a walker, a cane, or a motorized cart (they're called *mobies* here at Kimberly Hills), you can travel with ease and be part of everything that goes on. Generally, the connecting corridors are heated and air conditioned, a great conven-ience. But we visited one CCRC where, to our surprise, the walkways were outdoors and were merely covered arcades, open to the elements on the sides. That meant that in the Northeast winters one would need a coat to go from building to building and in the summer, the passage-ways could be sweltering.

Villas are not usually connected to the main building or buildings; they are commonly ranged along pleasant lanes and might be quite a distance from meals and activities. That can entail lovely walks in fine weather, short drives in poor—but what happens if you don't walk eas-ily and can't drive? A van will pick you up for meals, but it will do so when the van is ready, not necessarily when you are. For most other trips to the central building, you are on your own. Some of the villa res-idents here at Kimberly Hills rarely bother to travel to the dining room for dinner but prefer to order prepared meals from an outside gourmet market or cook at home. And in our time here, we have seen quite a few people give up their villas to move to apartments after becoming widowed or disabled, or when a spouse is moved to the health center and they want to be closer. One angle we never would have thought of until we lived here is that the people who want to move out of a villa generally are quite old and have been here a long time, perhaps a dozen or more years. Because of inflation over that period of time, entry fees have gone up steeply. One woman told us that although she would like to be in an apartment now, the entry fee is so much more than the refund she would get for her villa that she can't afford the move. Since there's no way to protect against this type of inflation, consider your future preferences, too.

Old friends, who are just about to move into a CCRC, decided on an apartment although they easily could have afforded a cottage. "We've *had* it with houses," they said. "We're looking forward to scaling down to a simpler life." But not everyone is so clear thinking. The cottage-apartment dilemma was part of our lengthy learning experience, and, in the end, we moved into a two-bedroom, two-bath apartment with a balcony and a gorgeous view of sunsets, distant hills, and a rose garden just below.

Our genuine pleasure in our home is something of a surprise, since we both feared that we would feel cramped in an apartment. And, in fact, it wasn't even our first choice. We had signed up for an apartment with two bedrooms and a den—a lovely little extra sitting room/ office/guestroom, enclosed on three sides by glass. But when it was time for us to move, the only available den apartment was unexpectedly snapped up by someone who was already a resident—and the rule is that residents have priority. There is no way we could have known until we were here how much time we would spend *out* of the apartment (dining, swimming, exercising, socializing, dancing, attending lectures or concerts, going shopping, and so on) and how well the space would work for us. Morton has his office in the second bedroom; mine is tucked into a corner of the master bedroom in front of a large bay window. Each of us has room for a computer, files, and plenty of bookshelves. And the bedroom is still a lovely bedroom. It even has an easy chair. The only disappointment is that I had planned to have a small piano in the den and now I have no room for one. I keep toying with the idea of getting an easy-to-stash-away electronic keyboard but find it hard to imagine that I would like it or consider it an adequate substitute for a real piano. Someday I'll get around to trying one so that I can form a real opinion.

ENTRY FEES AND MONTHLY CHARGES

After you have a good idea of how you want to live, it's time to consider cost, and this is a complex topic. The information you receive from the CCRC should be forthcoming with this type of information so you can make an informed decision. As previously noted, the common CCRC agreement requires the payment of an entry fee and a monthly fee thereafter. If you want to leave as large an estate as possible and the amount of the monthly fee is not a sticking point for you, look for a plan that provides a 100-percent refund. On the other hand, if it's important to keep your monthly costs down, and you don't need to boost your estate, a 50-percent refundable agreement will be better for you.

Check the literature to see whether the CCRCs you are considering offer the kind of plan you want. You can save a lot of time if you eliminate those that don't. (With regard to the refund, bear in mind that your entry fee doesn't earn interest. If you live for a long time, the amount you paid will be well eroded by inflation; even if you have a 100-percent refund, it may not be much of a boon to your estate.)

PUTTING TOGETHER YOUR CRITERIA LIST

When you've reviewed all the literature carefully and you think you are nearly ready to take things one step further and see for yourself what's out there, you can put together a short list of CCRCs to visit. The places you choose to see should, of course, offer those things that are most important to you. Everyone's standards are different, but to help you create your own list, here's a look at what our criteria list consisted of:

Organization
Non-profit only.

Certification
Certification by CCAC essential.

Location

Not more than two hours from New York City.
Suburban or rural setting with ample acreage.
Easy access to a city with museums, concerts,
and other public places and events.
Close to a university.

Health Care

Extensive contract only.
Medical clinic on premises.
All private rooms in nursing unit.
An assisted living unit.
An Alzheimer's unit.

Mission Statement

Assurance of life care.
A commitment to caring, compassionate, respectful
attention to all aspects of residents' well-being.

Aesthetics

Beautiful grounds with abundant open space.
Low-rise buildings with climate-controlled walkways
to main public areas.
A pleasant and gracious dining room.
An attractive coffee shop.

Residential Units

Two-bedroom, two-bath apartments with good layout,
generous rooms and storage.

Cost

An entry fee not to exceed the sale price of our house.
A monthly fee that will enable us to live comfortably
without fear of running out of money.

Essential Amenities

Swimming pool, fitness center and program, walking trails,
and classical music concerts.

Since we seriously considered only those CCRCs that fit these essential criteria, we wound up with a short list indeed. We selected eight places to visit. Some of them didn't work out for reasons already mentioned; we rejected others for such relatively trivial reasons as paper placemats and napkins in the dining room instead of linens, unattractive lobbies and/or corridors, and tacky kitchens or bathrooms. We passed on one because there was an eight-year waiting list. In the end, after we had visited all eight communities, Kimberly Hills just about chose itself. Due to the proliferation of available CCRCs around the country, you'll probably have many more to choose from.

CHAPTER 5

Visiting the Communities on Your List

W hen you've done all your homework, it's time to go see things for yourself. No matter how much information you have gathered, you can't possibly judge a CCRC without being there to see how it looks, feels, and smells. You have to meet the people—the staff and the residents—to get a sense of how comfortable you would be and whether you can see yourself really enjoying life there. You need to walk around, indoors and out, sit in the lounge, eat some meals, and get a feel for the ambience and a sense of the spirit of the community. It's helpful to look at people's faces and notice how they dress. Try to eavesdrop a little as they talk to one another and pay attention to the conversations they strike up—or don't—with you. Unless you are a devoutly practicing loner, you probably won't be drawn to a community where the residents are cliquish, cool to strangers, or non-communicative.

Casual encounters can leave lasting impressions. On one of our early CCRC visits we were greeted by a passing resident who spotted us as strangers. He introduced himself, we chatted a bit, and he asked if we would stay for dinner so that we could get better acquainted. Right then, he explained, he had to rush off because, as a retired physician, he was one of a group who volunteered to accompany residents to the hospital when they had to go for tests, procedures, or admission. "People are generally anxious," he said, "and it's very comforting to have a doctor friend along to explain the procedures, ask the right questions, and offer reassurance; sometimes we can even trot out the right buzzwords to cut through lots of red tape." How really wonderful! Our first impression was that this must be a warm, loving, caring community. And so it was. (We might have wound up there if the waiting list hadn't been so long.)

PLANNING OVERNIGHT VISITS

It is easy to plan a trip to look at a CCRC if it's in your own neighborhood or if you are planning to visit a single one. Keep in mind, however, that a single tour isn't the best idea, even if you're fairly sure you have already made your selection; if you haven't compared your choice to other places, you haven't made an *informed* choice. You owe it to yourself to know what's available, what you'd be getting that's special, or what you might be missing. Comparisons will either reinforce your choice or make you think about changing it. This is possibly the most important decision you're going to make from here on in, so it's worth some trouble to make sure it isn't wrong!

We were very enthusiastic about the first CCRC we visited, but with experience, we discovered that it fell short in many important respects, and almost all of what had impressed us most was common to all CCRCs. If you aren't staying close to home, try to save time and money by grouping two or three visits on a single trip, even if it takes several days. Many CCRCs will house and feed you without charge if you are coming from a distance.

Plan ahead because you can't just drop in, except for a casual look around. To see the place properly, you need to call and make an appointment for a tour; these are usually conducted only on weekdays and may be booked up for some days in advance. Allow plenty of time. It will take a bare minimum of two or three hours (unless you dislike the place at first sight and flee) for you to see everything and ask all your questions, and you will want to stay for at least one meal. If you can manage an overnight stay and several meals, that's ever so much better. When arranging your tour, ask the marketing director to plan meal dates with one or more residents for you, and ask if the facility has guest quarters where you can stay the night. This will give you the opportunity to hobnob a bit and to attend whatever evening programs are scheduled. Also, taking two or three meals instead of one gives you a chance to interact with more residents, get their inside information on what it's really like to live there, and form a more comprehensive assessment of the food and the dining facilities. You might even make some friends, as we did.

Since we were far from home and visiting two or three communities on a single trip, we sometimes found it most convenient to stay in a hotel that was central to all of our destinations and shuttle back and forth among them. There's too much to remember even when making a single visit, but combining two or more can get *really* confusing. It is vital to make meticulous notes about everything, even what seems obvious or trivial; without notes, you'll never remember which place had the overcooked vegetables or the gorgeous rose garden, where it was that the corridors were so ugly, or where the coffee was unbelievably good.

Overnight stays in the CCRC itself are useful for obvious reasons, although ours were not always as useful as we expected. However, we did have a variety of interesting experiences, both good and bad. One of our first "on premises" stays was at Holly Grove, and we were impressed with the elegantly furnished one-bedroom apartment they put us up in. For reasons I can't recall, although we had been told that a resident couple would be joining us for breakfast on our second day, no arrangements had been made for us to have companions for dinner the night we arrived. Not knowing where to go (and feeling somewhat shy), we fidgeted around our apartment until the designated dinner hour, then found our way to the dining room. We had been informed in advance that wine was welcome in the dining room so we had brought a bottle from home. The hostess had been notified of our arrival and was on the lookout for us; she greeted us warmly, then seated us at a large round table with five or six residents. We offered our wine and, of course, the larger-than-expected party made very quick work of the single bottle. We were amused by our very lively, jolly, and outgoing tablemates; they seemed to laugh a lot and were obviously having a great time. When dinner ended, one of the group suggested that we all repair to her apartment for after-dinner drinks. We never drink after dinner but were curious to see the woman's apartment and wanted to get better acquainted with the group, so we went. After a very short time, we began to realize that our ever-more-jolly new friends were, in fact, all decidedly sloshed. Their drinking party had obviously started long before we met them in the dining room. As they continued to imbibe and grow more and more boisterous, *we* grew more and more fidgety. Finally, pleading exhaustion due to our hard day and long trip, we managed to break away.

The next morning we kept our prearranged breakfast date with a particularly engaging and interesting couple. We felt at home with them immediately and told them about our experience of the evening before. They laughed and said, "Oh, you got mixed up with the *drinking* crowd! They spend two hours before dinner every night in the cocktail lounge." We realized that the innocent bottle of wine we were carrying to help break the ice with strangers must have given the efficient hostess a loud and unintended wrong signal.

At another CCRC, we stayed over on a Sunday night in order to take the tour on Monday morning. The only scheduled activity for the evening was vespers, conducted by a visiting minister and organist from a nearby church. The Sunday *New York Times* crossword puzzle is much more our Sunday-night habit than vespers, but since we had nothing else to do and were eager to participate in everything possible, we decided to look in. Mistake! Everyone in the room looked like Methuselah, and the hymn singing was thoroughly dispirited, off key, and remarkably dreary. But the good-natured minister and organist were working hard, and there were too few people in attendance for us to walk out without being very conspicuous, so we were trapped.

It was finally over, and just as we were gratefully escaping, a man nabbed us and introduced himself. After a few minutes of chat, he insisted that we return with him to his cottage to meet his wife and have coffee and cake. He seemed nice enough and it was still only eight o'clock, so we agreed. As soon as we had met his wife, our host, who turned out to be a retired minister, rushed to the phone and made a few calls. Before the coffee was ready, a half-dozen other residents had shown up. They were a totally different breed from the drowsy vespers group. These were dynamic people with interesting backgrounds, professions, and ideas. Their conversation was exciting and stimulating and we enjoyed them so much that we felt sure we would like to live among them. Unfortunately, we learned the following day that the CCRC had an eight-year waiting list for a two-bedroom apartment, so we dropped out in spite of finding so much to our liking. (There is an intentional warning here: Don't procrastinate! You can't make plans too early and you can always delay moving if you are called before you are ready).

TOURING AND TAKING NOTES

When you go on your scheduled tour, you will be shown all the public rooms, the special facilities like the swimming pool and fitness center, the ceramics and art studios, and the health center. You will also be able to visit one or more dwellings of the kind you have expressed interest in. Sometimes the way they are furnished makes it hard to see what they are really like. It is a common failing of CCRC residents to move in with the huge furniture they had always loved in their big house on the hill. In the new, smaller space it is too large, there is too much of it, and every surface is cluttered with too many "things." We saw living rooms that looked like furniture stores, and sideboards so crowded with china, silver, framed photos, and bric-a-brac that they looked like displays at a flea market. Conversely, we visited homes so exquisitely tasteful that they resembled photos in *Architectural Digest.* These apparently had been decorated by skilled professionals unhampered by tight budget restrictions. And many had lovely antiques of museum quality that had been handed down in the family for generations. (But of course, all our visits were in Connecticut or near Philadelphia, the heart of American antiques country!) Seeing how other people furnish is certainly educational. Either consciously or subliminally, and even with few heirlooms to worry about, I was constantly making mental notes: "Yes, this looks perfect, I must do it exactly that way" or "Good heavens, I have to be careful not to make a mistake like that."

But notes on paper are more useful than mental ones. Be sure to keep a small notebook in your pocket or purse at all times so that you can jot down random impressions, ideas, or questions as they occur. My little notebook traveled with me everywhere. Here's a sample of my entries:

Pass-through from kitchen to dining room is good! Standard? If not, can it be installed?

What's the story on glass shower doors? Installation permitted?

What about built-in bookshelves? Standard or extra?

Measure Grandma's walnut chest for fit on small wall near bedroom door.

Our dinner: mesclun salad (skimpy), grilled tuna (a little overcooked but not bad), baked potato, asparagus, good desserts. Six entrée choices: two each chicken, meat, fish; few veg.; pink table linen, fresh flowers, good china and flatware. Friendly college-student service.

How far to airport?

Bus to concerts in the city?

In addition to your notebook, you will (I hope) have a copy of the Checklist for Comparing CCRCs in Appendix A. Be sure to include a blank page for any additional items that are of special interest to you. (You, might, for example, consider it essential that there be lap lanes in the swimming pool, that the coffee shop be open before seven in the morning, or that your grandchildren can visit you for a month at a time.) Not only will the checklist help you to keep the details straight, it will prompt you to ask questions you might otherwise forget.

Take along a camera, too. You don't need to be a skilled photographer, just able to peer through the viewfinder and push the little button. Pictures are absolutely invaluable, so if you don't own a camera, buy a disposable one for each trip. Even if you visit only a single CCRC, you will be unable to remember many of the details you can capture on film. If you visit more than one, I promise you that they will blur and blend together and you'll never know which one had those big casement windows. When I looked at the photos I took, I saw many details I hadn't noticed before, not even while I was taking the pictures.

I also found it useful to carry a measuring tape on all the tours to supply important information when assessing our collected findings after we were back home. The printed floor plans give gross room dimensions but most often they are not strictly to scale and won't tell you the length of that bit of wall between the window and the corner, or the space between the entrance and the closet. If you are seriously interested in a particular villa or apartment, jot down such measurements right on the floor plan; you will be glad you did when you begin to wonder where, or if, your furniture will fit.

If you are a kitchen person, take photos of all four kitchen walls to remind you of how many cabinets there are. This *might* minimize your tendency to bring two or three times as much equipment as you can house—or will ever use. (It didn't work for me. I took plenty of pictures but still have fifteen kinds of cake pans and huge platters suited to parties the dining area could never hold. But what might I have brought *without* the pictures?) Also, make note of the other kitchen features. Is the space well lighted? Attractive and well equipped? Is there a dishwasher? Ice-maker? Garbage disposal? Adequate counter space? Good stove, oven, and refrigerator? Are improvements permitted?

Make careful note, too, of any potential extra storage space you see. Our apartment has a very narrow utility room for the heating and air-conditioning equipment, and we measured every inch of its free space. It turned out that, as skinny as the closet is, it just manages to accommodate a small chest of drawers and eight feet of shallow but tall shelf units we had used for basement storage and were going to throw out before we moved. The chest holds table linens and assorted odds and ends, the shelves store *everything* from laundry soap to simple tools, gift wrap, vases, baskets, cookbooks, light bulbs, furniture polish, toys for visiting children, miscellaneous junk, and yes, the cake pans and platters. We often refer to the closet as "the basement."

If you see the kind of living unit you would like to have, find out how long you might have to wait for one. Obviously, since the turnover is usually dependent on residents' deaths or permanent moves to the health center, no one can predict accurately when a particular unit will become available, but management can usually make an educated guess. (See "Signing on to the Waiting List" below.)

Small apartments are easier to come by than larger ones. There may be variations in other parts of the country, but in all the CCRCs we visited (none of which had studios, although they exist elsewhere), one-bedroom apartments were the easiest to get. As the CCRC idea has caught on, many more couples than anticipated are moving in, and even single people, if they can afford it, often want an extra room for

SIGNING ON TO THE WAITING LIST

Be sure to find out if there is a waiting list for the living unit you want and how long the wait is likely to be. Don't be surprised if it is years. If you are at all interested, sign on to the waiting list, even if you still have other CCRCs to visit and won't be ready to move for a long time. You have little to lose and much to gain. (There is one caveat, however: If you develop a serious illness while you are on the waiting list, the CCRC can turn you down at the very last minute. Be sure to ask about this.)

To be included on the waiting list, you will have to fill out some forms and leave a deposit, usually $1,000–$2,000, all but a small part of which is refundable if you change your mind. (But ask! Remember the $1,000 we inadvertently contributed to Holly Grove.)

You have probably guessed that you are never going to find a place that has absolutely everything. Making a decision is a complex process and, in the end, you might be glad to be on the waiting list somewhere that you mentally wrote off initially as being less than perfect. We looked at Kimberly Hills fairly early in our search, saw several communities that we liked better for one reason or another, but in the end, as we learned more and were better able to judge what was truly important to us, Kimberly won out over all the others on a point-for-point basis.

Once you are on a waiting list, you are usually given certain privileges. These may include use of some of the facilities (such as the fitness center and pool), some free dinners, invitations to special events, regular mailings of the newsletters, and other perks.

an office, studio, or guestroom. It is not unusual for people to move into a one-bedroom apartment while they wait for a larger one or a cottage to become available. Once you're a resident, you usually have precedence over nonresidents on the waiting list. But be sure to find out if that's the case and if moving up is permitted; we visited two CCRCs that sanctioned moves to smaller quarters, but not to larger ones.

While you are discussing availability, try to think in terms of specific exposures and locations and add these to your criteria. A given floor plan can be more or less desirable, depending on where it is located on the grounds. We found that out the hard way.

We were unable to get the apartment we wanted by the closing date for our house sale, so we were relieved and happy that there was a two-bedroom coming up and we wouldn't be homeless. Here at Kimberly—and probably everywhere—as soon as an apartment is vacant, it is painted, newly carpeted, and everything is put into sparkling, as-new condition. When we went to see ours, we were carrying the floor plan with cutouts of all our furniture glued in place, and we couldn't wait to make our new home a reality. We were thrilled with what we saw and were eager to get going.

So we moved. Having little grasp of the confusing interior geography of the Kimberly buildings until we actually lived there, we were surprised to discover that we were nearly as far as it was possible to get from the central building. And that was far! What with going to dinner, to the mailroom, the bank, fitness center, or pool, we walked several miles a day. Good exercise, we thought—but what happens if, one day, we can't walk that much? We noticed that a number of residents along our hall buzzed back and forth in mobie carts, although once they got to their destination, they seemed able to walk perfectly well. Aha! They could walk, *but not that far.* Maybe that location was not so good for the future.

But there was another aspect of our location that soon began to bother us in the present—all our windows faced north. Although we had a lovely view, we never saw the sun or the moon. We were used to living in a house with lots of glass doors, many windows, skylights, and clerestories. We lived with the celestial bodies, basked in sunshine and moonlight, and our days and nights were tuned to the rhythm of nature. I began to feel, in my north-facing home, as if something elemental and essential was missing from my life. It was starting to make me unhappy.

Not surprisingly, when we moved into Kimberly Hills, we were sure that we had moved for the last time and would *never* have to do it again. We reminded each other of that frequently as we slogged through unpacking the endless boxes, arranging cabinets, sorting books, hanging pictures, finding places for things, making our nest. About the time it was all completed to our satisfaction, we put in a request for a different apartment. Six months from the time we had arrived, we moved again.

As moves go, it wasn't so bad. There were no decisions to make, we took everything and put it all in the same place since the apartment layout was the same. What was wonderfully different was our western exposure with a flood of afternoon sunshine and moonlight streaming through the bedroom windows at night. And here we are a relatively short walk away from everything we need to get to. (No mobies on *this* hall.) There are even laundry and trash rooms right across the corridor, where they couldn't be handier. By now, we have nearly forgotten all the pains (physical as well as emotional) of moving, love our new apartment, and would do it all over again if we had to. But then, if we could do it all over again, we wouldn't need to because we would have made a more informed choice in the first place.

INSPECTING THE HEALTHCARE FACILITIES

Although finding exactly the right apartment or villa is undoubtedly a primary factor in choosing a CCRC, keep your eye on the *most* important matter, the only reason you're thinking CCRC in the first place: This move is all about health care.

Here, on your tour, you can find out everything the brochure does not tell you. You can spend time inspecting the health facilities, get a copy of the healthcare agreement, and ask the marketing director all your questions. It helps if you know what the questions are. (Use the checklist in Appendix A!)

First, visit the health center and pay careful attention. I was surprised (at first) to learn that many visitors to Kimberly Hills prefer not to see the health facilities at all or, if they are urged to visit, rush through as quickly as possible. But on reflection, I realized that we are all reluctant to enter hospitals and sickrooms. We are made uncomfortable by the sight of people who aren't well, and even more uncomfortable by the thought that we might become sick ourselves. But try hard to overcome your reluctance and denial and realize that *this is why you're here.* This is the part of the facility that you're going to be paying all that big money for.

Your first impression will probably be accurate and is important. Does the facility look attractive and cheerful? Is it clean? Does it *smell* clean? (This is major!) Is there plenty of help and do they appear to be warm and friendly? Where doors are open, peep in. The patients won't mind; the open door is an invitation and people here are used to visitors. Are the rooms private? Attractive and personalized? Are the patients clean and tidy with clean, combed hair? If they aren't bedridden, are they properly dressed? Difficult as it is to do, try to picture yourself here. Would you feel cared for, protected, and comfortable— or would you feel jailed? This is a tough thing to ask of you, but try to do it. You might be surprised at the different responses different places elicit, and that's important information for you to take away.

In addition to the skilled nursing unit, you will want to look at the assisted-living quarters and the Alzheimer's unit.

Here are some of the questions to keep in mind or ask while touring the healthcare facilities:

- Are all the rooms private, with private bath, or is there an extra charge for privacy?

- Is the facility certified for Medicare reimbursement? For Medicaid?

- Is there an adequate assisted-living unit? (This is for people who don't need skilled nursing care but require assistance with some daily activities such as bathing, dressing, or taking medications.) Are the assisted-living quarters apartments or single rooms? Are they attractive? (Here at Kimberly, they are apartments, lacking only a kitchen.)

- Is there a special Alzheimer's unit? Are any restraints used? What kinds of programs are offered? Are there support groups for families?

- Is there an attractive lounge area and dining room in the healthcare facility?

- What is the ratio of registered nurses to patients? Of certified nurses' aides? (Look in the Resources section for the Medicare website that supplies this, and other, information.)

DISCUSSING YOUR HEALTHCARE CONTRACT

When you have finished your tour of the health center, and it's still fresh in your mind, it might be the right time to sit down in the marketing office, rest your feet, and discuss the healthcare contract, or agreement (both terms are used). If only the extensive agreement is offered, read it through and inquire about anything that isn't crystal clear. What happens to your residence if you move to the health center? What happens if you need a bed and they are all taken? Will you ever be required to hire private help if you are in the health center? If there is a choice of agreements, make sure you understand the distinctions among them. When you have asked the questions that occur to you, ask for a copy of the agreement to take home so you can study it at length and at leisure. It takes a long time to do a thorough job and, if you like what you see, you will want your lawyer to see it, too.

To reiterate, an extensive agreement will give you housing, some meals, amenities, and all the care you ever need without substantial additional charge. There may be minor charges for extra meals or some kinds of medical supplies. Modified agreements cover housing, some meals, amenities, and a specified number of nursing-care days per year. When those days have been used up, there is a daily charge. Fee-for-service agreements give you housing, meals, and amenities, but do not cover any healthcare services. Health care is paid for at the prevailing rates when it is needed. These agreements are attractive to those who want lower entry and monthly fees, but there is always the risk that inflation will run up the cost of services to a prohibitive level. Even with long-term-care insurance, costs could rise beyond the policy's coverage unless it has adequate inflation protection.

You will also want to know what kind of *routine* health care is available. Are there doctors on the premises? Do you have to use those doctors? What are their credentials? Are they specialists in geriatrics? What hospitals are they affiliated with? Can you walk into the clinic without an appointment if you suddenly have a problem? Are prescription drugs provided without charge (very rare these days)? Are medications provided on the premises? What kinds of specialists are available? Is there always a nurse on call? Will the CCRC provide transportation to outside medical appointments? Is there a physical therapy office on the premises? A dental office? A visiting psychiatrist, audiologist, dermatologist, podiatrist, or other specialists? If you activate the emergency call system from your home (every CCRC provides them), who responds? How fast?

This is a good time to discuss your medical insurance. Presumably, you have or will have Medicare and a supplement, or Medigap, policy. Find out what kind of supplementary insurance the CCRC requires you to carry. At the time of this writing, all Medigap policies are designated by the letters "A" through "J," and they all have exactly the same coverage for each category, but costs may vary. Most CCRCs will require that you maintain at least a "C" policy.

Although you will need to maintain supplementary insurance, you may find that it's possible to change to a much less expensive policy. Some CCRCs pay for all or part of your prescription drugs and, if that is what the literature states, you may not need pharmacy coverage. (But check! If there is prescription-drug coverage, find out if it's unlimited or if there is an annual maximum and, very important, if this is subject to change.) Another consideration involves taxes. If your CCRC meets certain IRS criteria, you can take a large medical deduction off your income tax since a portion of all the fees you pay is earmarked for health care. The criteria are complex but they go something like this: The CCRC has to guarantee you care for as long as you live. You have to be capable of independent living when you move in. While you do not need long-term care immediately, you are guaranteed such care when and if you do need it and for as long as you need it. And there will not be any substantial charges for health or nursing care at any time.

Some aspects of the law are unclear, so be sure to ask your tax adviser—which you will do before making a decision, in any case. But if you choose a non-profit CCRC with an extensive contract, it is likely that all the criteria will be met. We knew they would be met at Kimberly Hills, but were pleasantly astonished (for once!) when tax time rolled around to learn that we were entitled to a 41-percent deduction on both our entry fee and our monthly fees for the first year. A truly

IMPUTED TAX

After we foolishly signed on to the waiting list at Holly Grove, we asked for a copy of their contract to take home and review. It was there that we saw, for the first time, that term *imputed tax*. We had no idea what it meant and had a very hard time trying to find out. No one at the CCRC offered an explanation that we could understand. But now we do understand, and the concept isn't really difficult at all. Here's how it works:

When you pay an entry fee to a CCRC that does not meet the IRS criteria mentioned on page 57, and if that fee is refundable, the IRS can deem you to have made a non-interest-bearing loan to the establishment. Come tax time, you'll owe the IRS tax on the interest you would have earned on the money if you had made a loan at the market rate, which is set by the IRS each year. Some portion of the entry fee is exempt from the tax, and the law is not yet fully defined, so if you run into the term *imputed tax* anywhere, be sure to consult your tax adviser.

nice surprise. In subsequent years, the deduction has been even higher, up to 46 percent last year. And, unless you have a very high income, such a large deduction will raise you to the IRS threshold that allows you to deduct all your other medical costs as well—dental care, eyeglasses, hearing aids, and so forth. While we're on the subject of taxes, let me keep my earlier promise and tell you more about imputed tax (see "Imputed Tax" above).

If you have gotten this far with your visit, filled in your checklist, and made notes about it all, you probably need a break. So why not go to lunch and, in the next chapter, we'll discuss your dining experience. We'll also look into all the other services and amenities you will still need to check out before you can conclude your visit and head for home.

CHAPTER 6

Checking Out the Amenities

menities are what make all the difference between adequate shelter and a gracious lifestyle, the kind that makes you feel actively good and glad to be where you are. Your future home's amenities will play a major role in your day-to-day contentment, so assessing what a CCRC has to offer deserves your time and attention.

The big things are out of the way—you have gotten your general impression, looked at the living units, and visited the health center—and now you can focus on all those little things that add up to the pleasures and satisfactions of daily life.

FOOD SERVICE AND THE DINING EXPERIENCE

Of all the amenities, none is more important for health, pleasure, and overall satisfaction than food. You are probably muttering that food is a *necessity*, not an amenity, and so it is. Every CCRC will feed you, but with what kind of food? Sustenance food keeps you going but doesn't make you happy. The amenity kind is fresh, tasty, and of good quality. It is creatively and expertly prepared, and beautifully served in attractive surroundings. Mealtime is a social and pleasurable time—a time to relax, to meet with friends, to exchange ideas and chitchat, to savor delicious food, to linger over a cup of coffee, and to feel good. Particularly in retirement, a fine dinner is often the high point of the day.

At CCRCs, anywhere from one to three meals are included in the monthly fee; the most common arrangement provides one (dinner is the obvious choice), with the other two available at extra charge. When you have a meal during your visit, you will sample the food of a single lunch or dinner, and it may or may not be representative of all the meals served there. If you can, ask some residents how they like the food. You might also ask to see dinner menus for the past week or two to check on how much variety there is and whether the selections are attractive to you.

As you dine, you will be able to assess the food itself, the aesthetics of the dining room and/or coffee shop, the competency and courtesy of the wait staff, and the hours of service.

Criteria differ, so you will make your own personal judgments about what you like and what you don't. As mentioned, one CCRC that we visited used paper placemats and napkins and served grocery-store white bread. The entire experience was too reminiscent of summer camp and we disliked it intensely, but those who live there seemed perfectly happy. There is no arguing with taste. I readily admit that when it comes to food, my standards are high. Simply put, I just love a really fine meal!

Kimberly Hills, like most of the other CCRCs we visited, has a spacious and nicely furnished dining room, similar to the dining room in a good hotel. It looks very civilized. There is crisp linen, decent china and silverware, a pleasant wait staff, and we may come in for dinner up until 7:30 PM (We visited several communities with a 6 PM limit—our usual cocktail hour—and dining that early would have required more of an adjustment than we were willing to make.) Kimberly's menu is very impressive—at first—since it has a number of choices of soups, salads, appetizers, entrées, and desserts. But we soon learned that it is very repetitious. (In honesty, not everyone finds it so.) Since we eat little meat, like an abundance of fresh vegetables, and shun fried and fatty foods, we have limited choices and get more variety at home. There are others who love the dining room and go every night. I like to cook and I cook what we like, so most nights we eat at home and sometimes go out to restaurants.

In fairness, I would probably tire of my favorite restaurant if I went there every night, but a CCRC, with its captive clientele, needs to make a special effort to provide good variety. I don't know if any of them do, but maybe you'll find out in your travels. If you have any special dietary needs—if, for example, you are a vegetarian—determine whether the menu will accommodate you adequately. Ask, too, if special menus can be arranged for medical conditions such as diabetes or high cholesterol. (Here at Kimberly, you are pretty much on your own with special diets unless you are in the health center.)

Make sure you find out what the dress code is. The Kimberly dining room requires a jacket and tie for men, and "proper" dress for women—that is, no shorts or blue jeans, although dress slacks are fine. During the summer months, men are permitted to forgo the ties, but still must wear jackets.

When assessing the dining-room situation at a potential CCRC, other important considerations include:

- Are you permitted to bring wine to the dining room? (At Kimberly we are, and often do, and the server opens the bottle and provides glasses.)

- What are the guest rules? Is there a limit to how many guests you can have at one meal? In a month? How much do you have to pay for guest meals? If you don't use up your allotted thirty meals in the month, can you use them for guests? (We can.)

- Is there a separate dining room where you can have a private party? (At Kimberly, there is a very elegant space, but it is available only if you use Kimberly catering. Not many residents take advantage of this; I suspect more people would if outside catering were permitted.)

More important for many people than the formal dining room is the coffee shop or informal dining room. Here, there is no dress code, so you can come as you are in your khakis and sweater or sundress. Getting dressed up for dinner is fun some of the time, but not seven nights a week (although some people here seem to love it). Kimberly's coffee shop is quite typical in that it has a large salad bar and cafeteria service. The ambience is pleasant for dining, and take-out service, a popular option, is provided for what Morton and I call "the basket brigade." There is also a lovely outdoor dining terrace with umbrella-covered tables for warm-weather use and a mini convenience store for milk, eggs, bread, orange juice, and the like.

One of the challenges (for me, anyway) of community living is that it can easily feel too institutional. Dining at home, as we did formerly, minimizes this substantially. I happen to like to cook (hardly anyone here does), so I often make our entire dinner. Sometimes, I make one favorite dish—a hearty soup, chicken, fish, or pasta, perhaps—then we fetch a few things from the coffee shop like salad greens, baked potatoes, or maybe an entrée. There are good breads available, as well as a variety of desserts and beverages.

An important question to ask is whether meals will be delivered to you if you aren't feeling well—or even if you are but would just rather stay home. Some communities offer "room service" for a small fee.

I suggest that you make extensive notes on food and food service in your notebook. It may seem trivial to you now, but there is nothing that arouses more comment and discussion in a CCRC than the food. Whether the green beans were overcooked or undercooked can become a hot topic of the day.

THE FITNESS CENTER
AND SPORTING OPPORTUNITIES

After all that emphasis on eating, it's time to think about exercise. You should expect to find a good fitness center with plenty of up-to-date machines and at least one professional trainer. Even if you have never been in an exercise program before, you might become a convert, as I did. In my "former life" I swam a lot and played tennis, so I had a rather disdainful opinion of exercise by machine. But Kimberly's state-of-the-art fitness center seduced me. With a personal trainer who constantly pushed my limits, I soon took pride in doing my mile on the treadmill before starting out to set new limits on all the strength machines or ostentatiously curling my 12-pound dumbbells. I had expected it to be boring, but I came to enjoy the convivial clubbiness of the gym. Even if fitness training doesn't appeal to you now, think of it as part of your future health care. We have seen many very frail elderly people become amazingly more robust and limber with supervised exercise.

Not ready to give up our favorite sports, a pool and access to a tennis court were criteria for us during our search. The pool here is indoors and adequate in size, although I wish it were outside and much larger. There is also a Jacuzzi, which we enjoyed the week we moved in and were nothing but aching muscles from strenuous unpacking. (Oddly enough, we haven't used it since.)

There are nearby tennis courts in town that we use in season. Kimberly has a nine-hole putting green that is much used (though not by us), a fancy croquet court (likewise), and sixty acres for walking. Few CCRCs have full golf courses, but if golf is your passion, you might want to inquire about privileges at a nearby club or public park. No matter which is your sport, ask if there are extra charges for using the facilities and whether there are organized tournaments or other events you would enjoy.

HOBBIES

If arts and crafts are your hobbies, you might discover that with your reduced floor space there isn't room for your loom, kiln, easel, or whatever, so investigate what's offered in your line. Here at Kimberly, there is an elegant art studio with excellent lighting and plenty of work and storage space. My husband paints, and I very much appreciate (he does, too, of course) the fact that all his considerable painting gear lives in the studio, not in our apartment. Since the studio is never closed, he goes whenever the mood seizes him, and, once a week, he attends a morning art class there. At Kimberly, we also have a complete woodworking shop, which is very well stocked by all the residents who brought their tools along with them when they moved in. Many other CCRCs have ceramic workshops.

ENTERTAINMENT

Good entertainment is part of the good life, and in a CCRC, it is important to have frequent on-site programs for the benefit of those who don't get around much anymore. Here, we have a wealth of activities. One can play organized bridge (rubber and duplicate), attend lectures of every description, movies, concerts, dance groups, and cocktail dancing—there is always something going on. There is no charge for these in-house events. In addition, there is bus transportation to the

Philadelphia Orchestra concerts (it is *so* nice not to have to park), to plays and operas, museums, movies, points of interest, even trips lasting several days to various vacation spots. Yes, you can drive now, but maybe one day you won't be able to, and think about how important it will be not to be shut yourself off from outside life. A wealth of cultural, educational, and just plain fun programs is vital. So are daily convenience trips to shopping and outside medical and dental appointments, and Sunday trips to nearby houses of worship.

MISCELLANEOUS AMENITIES

Among other amenities to look for are a bank on the premises, a beauty/barber shop, meeting and game rooms, a gift shop, indoor parking, resident gardens and greenhouse, guest accommodations, good storage space outside your residence (to make up for the basement and attic you are going to miss), and good laundry facilities. There should be a staff of handy-persons to make minor repairs, help you move furniture, or even change hard-to-reach light bulbs. Although not an amenity in the traditional sense, be sure to inquire if pets are permitted if this is important to you. At Kimberly, a resident may have two pets. Dogs generally must submit to an "interview" to make sure they are friendly.

One of the amenities at Kimberly is a handsome reading/computer room. There is a wide selection of current periodicals and local newspapers as well as *The New York Times* and *The Wall Street Journal*. Two computers with broadband Internet service are available for anyone's use and free instruction is offered. When we first moved here, we were among a handful of people with our own computers, but now, within a few years, a large number of residents who learned the basics in the reading room have acquired computers and gone online on their own.

THE RESIDENTS' ASSOCIATION

Find out if there is a residents' association at the CCRC, how much power it has, and how it functions. It should play a vital role in governing the community and serve to give every resident a voice in the democratic process. Here, the residents' association supports the vast number of committees that enable all of us to volunteer and participate in areas of our expertise, special interest, or personal choice. Resident committees run the gift and thrift shops, the lectures, movies, classical music concerts, and other such events, and serve in an advisory capacity to certain administrative areas like decorating and dining. Outside of such endeavors, the Residents' Association has no real power.

WINDING UP YOUR TOUR AND LAST-MINUTE DETAILS

Before you end your visit, ask for copies of the in-house events calendar and newsletter or magazine. These can give you a pretty good feel for who these people are, what their interests are, what they do, and what the general character of the place is.

Ask, too, for a copy of the contract or agreement and the publication that lists the rules and regulations. It is here, in the fine print, that you can really find out the details of what you will be buying into. You will get the answers to questions you would never think to ask, including: What happens if a resident couple gets divorced? And if one of them wants to marry a person below the eligible age for the community? But it also has answers to questions you *should* have asked but probably didn't: What are the financial arrangements when one spouse is in the health center but the other remains in the residence? What is the history of increases in monthly charges? If a friend or family member

AN IMPORTANT REMINDER!

It is essential to keep meticulous notes and take lots of photos. Even if you have the memory of a gifted elephant, you can't possibly remember every detail. As soon as you have visited two CCRCs, they will blur together in your mind and you won't be able to remember which place had which feature. Make quick annotations on your checklist (see Appendix A) and enter as much additional information as possible into your notebook. Don't fail to enter the first items on the checklist, which include the marketer's e-mail address and phone and fax numbers; if the place is one that interests you, you will want to ask the many questions that keep popping up once you're back at home.

wants to come for a visit, how long may he or she stay? What kind of health insurance are you required to maintain? What are the tax benefits, if any? What happens if you run out of money?

Speaking of money, be sure to get a copy of the Disclosure Statement; you will want to show it to your lawyer and accountant along with the agreement.

It was comparing all the fine print that caused us to reject two other CCRCs that seemed, on the surface, to be more our style. But Kimberly's fine print knocked the others out of the competition. It was far and away the best deal when we focused on our bottom line. This isn't just for now, we reminded ourselves over and over again, it's for when we're sick and health care is the major issue.

And that's what this is all about, right? It's why we did what we did and why you're reading this book.

CHAPTER 7

Taking the Plunge

Months or years may have passed since you first began to consider a CCRC, but now you've done it. You've made your choice, the residence you've chosen has become available, and this is the moment when you have to put your house on the market or give your landlord notice. (This is the scary moment when I couldn't eat or sleep, and you might have the same experience.)

The logistics of accomplishing the move may seem absolutely insurmountable—but they aren't. I ask you to accept this as a matter of faith because I live with some three hundred other people who all felt as you do now, and every single one of them managed to do what had to be done, and they all survived.

If you are a homeowner rather than a renter, you may be counting on the proceeds from the house sale to pay your entry fee. If so, *before* you sign your CCRC contract ask if the management will give you a bridge loan until the sale closes. They generally will, and at a reasonable rate of interest. Otherwise, you will either have to come up with the cash or wait until your house sale closes and hope that the living unit you picked out will still be available for you. Ask your CCRC marketing director for advice and help with this step; it's in their best interest to be accommodating.

Since you will probably be moving from a larger to a smaller space, one of the most daunting tasks of the transition is scaling down your possessions. This means getting rid of everything you don't absolutely need. You may also have to downsize some things you *do* need. If your big sectional sofa will overwhelm your new living room, get rid of it and buy a smaller one. It may help to picture the rooms dismayingly stuffed with mansion-sized furniture and tons of bric-a-brac you saw when you were on your CCRC tour.

On request, your CCRC will most likely provide you with a large floor plan and scaled-to-size cutouts of furniture so that you can easily see what fits gracefully. You can also use graph paper and store-bought or homemade cutouts that are carefully measured to conform to your own furniture. Remember that visual clutter, such as too many pictures or objects, can make you feel as crowded as too much furniture.

There is also a strong psychic factor here so that people have different perceptions of clutter. Some folks feel most comfortable and cozy surrounded by a lot of "stuff." I tend to the other extreme and need wide open spaces, and it was immediately obvious to me that most of our furniture was simply too big for the new apartment. Without a pang, we gave our big stripped pine harvest table and chairs to a granddaughter (she and her husband were just moving to a country house, a brilliant stroke of luck for us!). We were able to sell our two large sofas to the house buyer; we didn't get a big price, but it was another problem solved. We bought one medium-sized sofa and a really small dining table with drop leaves. We also parted with a four-foot round coffee table and bought a slender, rectangular one. We gave away hundreds of books to the library, a charity, and friends; I gave almost all the professional books that lined the walls of my therapy office to two colleagues just starting out in private practice. It gives us the greatest pleasure to visit the grandchildren and find some of our familiar furniture, like old friends, in their homes. As for books, we sometimes search the shelves for volumes that aren't there, occasionally replace one, but, for the most part, we don't remember what we gave away; books come and go and life doesn't change as a result.

The only thing I truly hated to part with was my wonderful piano, a Steinway grand, model A, not even a remotely possible fit in the new digs. But although it was a wrench, the parting went smoothly. I happened to see a Steinway ad in the paper seeking good used Steinway pianos. I called, they sent a technician who took the piano apart and put it back together again, then made an offer. We probably could have gotten more from a private buyer but only after a number of "lookers" came to play Czerny or "Für Elise." And that seemed onerous at a time when we were so busy. So we accepted Steinway's offer but said that we didn't have a moving date yet and would let them know when to pick it up. "No problem," said Steinway, "just tell us when you're ready." A day or two later, to my great surprise, a check for the full purchase price arrived in the mail. Weeks passed before we had a set moving date, and then I called to tell Steinway to pick up the piano. And I called, and I called. Only when I said that we were down to the wire and ready to leave did they finally send the truck.

A car, or cars, called for another decision. Although we had always had two, a necessity in the country, we decided that we would try to get along with one, so we sold the older one, and that was a good decision. With neither of us going out to work, one car is perfectly adequate, and it reduced our expenses considerably. We do careful scheduling, telling each other when we will need the car for a dental appointment or a trip to the mall. We have no conflict.

The last part of the clearing-out process was a managed tag sale. We engaged a local antiques dealer who came two days beforehand with a SWAT team to tag every piece of furniture, set up tables to display china, pictures, small appliances, rugs, silver, vases, lamps—all the things that we had accumulated over time. It was terribly strange and disorienting, so we decided to absent ourselves from the sale. Droves of people came, lots of things were sold, a few items (silver and jewelry) were stolen, and then it was over. The dealer took on consignment a few good things that were left—a silver tea service, three small oriental rugs, a violin—and all the rest was given away to a charity thrift shop.

We hired a man with a truck to clean out whatever remained in the basement, and he carted many loads to the library, the thrift shop, and the dump. It sounds drastic, and I guess it was, but the truth is that I never missed anything except my piano and my food processor. (The latter was easy to replace, and I like the new one better.) When all was said and done, we still kept too much.

Throughout the clearing-out process, both of us were looking ahead, not back. We were excited about going to Kimberly, equally eager and apprehensive. It was, after all, a leap into the unknown, a whole new, different, strange way of life. Even after all our careful planning, we wondered if we would really like it, if we would fit in, if we would find new friends, if we had done the right thing. Sometime during those last months and weeks, we noticed that our clothes were all but falling off and discovered that each of us had lost ten pounds!

Because our home in East Hampton was a five-hour drive from Kimberly, we made long-distance arrangements to get a few things done before the move to ease our transition. By phone, we arranged for an extra phone line to be installed in the apartment and also for a window-treatment worker to measure and make blinds for the bedroom windows. Kimberly's moving coordinator let the workmen in, and she even accepted delivery of the new, smaller furniture we had ordered. Going by the floor plan we had faxed to her office, she had the deliverymen place the new furniture exactly where we wanted it. We had done everything we could think of. Now all we had to do was get there.

*   *   *

Despite our sleepless nights and jittery days imagining all the things that could go wrong, nothing did. The move was amazingly smooth. The packers came on a Monday and packed everything except the linens on our bed, our overnight bag, and a few odds and ends. We had dinner with friends, stayed out as late as possible, and then returned to our spooky, packed-up house.

Somehow, Tuesday morning finally arrived, and the moving van pulled into the driveway at the crack of dawn. It was all loaded by early afternoon. Because the trip was a long one and the van was not permitted on the parkways, it would start out for Kimberly Hills on Wednesday morning.

But Morton and I were set to go and couldn't wait to get moving. Although the closing on our house wouldn't take place for several days, we had gone to our lawyer's office, signed all the papers, left a deposit slip so the secretary could take the check right to our bank, arranged for the house to be thoroughly cleaned, and set forth to greet our new life. We hadn't entrusted our two computers to the movers so they filled almost the entire back of our small car. The interstices held a few choice paintings and various articles of clothing on hangers topped off the heap. We looked like a still from the movie *Grapes of Wrath*.

We arrived at our new home in the early evening exhausted, exhilarated, and apprehensive. It was really, really strange. We drove into the garage, parked in our assigned slot for the first time, and picked up the large rolling cart we had arranged to have waiting for us. We piled on the computers and the rest of our things, and trundled it all into the elevator. We didn't see a soul or hear a sound, and within a minute or two, there we were, standing in our new home with a pile of computer monitors, mini towers, printers, and tangles of cable. There were no overhead lights in the apartment since we had requested that the dining-area chandelier be removed, and of course, our lamps had not yet arrived. Fortunately, there was a flashlight in the car.

In the master bedroom, we found two folding beds nicely made up (but hideously uncomfortable, as it turned out) and one lamp. We took turns using the lamp to hook up our computers, our first step toward settling in, so that we would feel in touch with the outside world.

A hopeful peek into the refrigerator was rewarded by a lovely Kimberly welcome basket holding a fine cold dinner. Having had lots of time to make plans during all those long nights, we had brought a bottle of wine and, yes, a corkscrew and two glasses. So we sat down on the floor with our picnic, smothered by new-carpet smell, and toasted ourselves for having actually pulled it off. We had been three years in the process.

After another wide-eyed, jittery night, we had an early breakfast in the coffee shop and returned to our empty apartment to fidget some more. But we didn't have to fidget for long. To our delight, the movers had started out in the middle of the night and arrived with all our worldly goods at 10 AM. They propped open the door while they brought things in and, in the course of the hubbub, several passing neighbors stopped in to welcome us and offer help of every kind. That was nice! They all introduced themselves but by that night we were dismayed to realize that we had already forgotten all their names. Since it was clear that we would soon be dealing with hundreds of names and probably forgetting them all, we decided to keep a written list of all the people we met. It was very helpful. Meeting so many people at once is monumentally confusing, but we soon learned that since everyone had gone through it, no one took it amiss when we forgot who they were.

By the time the movers left, we were surrounded by so many boxes that there was virtually no room to unpack them, so we finally gave up; we took showers and dressed (courtesy of the overnight bag), and nervously made our way to the dining room. There, the hostess asked if we would like to be seated with another couple, we said we would, and then and there began our new social life.

The next morning, while we were still floundering around in chaos, two of our children arrived, and amazingly, they unpacked the entire kitchen—dishes, pots, bowls, the works. It was a big step. With their help we managed to shelve some of the books and unload the wardrobe containers into closets. We began to feel as if order were possible, if still distant, and we were encouraged. It wasn't until the next day, trying to make breakfast, that I realized that I had no idea where to find anything in the kitchen and would have to rearrange it all according to my own system before it could feel like home.

We learned belatedly that wherever there are CCRCs, there are companies that specialize in unpacking, setting up, and making order. When we made our second move a few months later, we used such an outfit and it was a colossal help. They came early and packed, the movers came and moved it all, then the packers-unpackers did their job with dispatch. They removed all the boxes, even vacuumed up the mess, and by dinnertime we were spic and span and in perfect order (although once again, we had to reorganize the kitchen and reshelve the books). When you're ready to make your move, ask your CCRC for a referral if you want that kind of help.

During the next few days we finished unpacking, hanging pictures, and trying to decide where to put things. We worked until we were too sore to move, then we went and sat in the Jacuzzi and let the hot water pound our aching backs.

Because we were in a totally strange situation, we had a number of adjustment problems that people from the neighborhood don't have. And the majority of people do stay in their own neighborhood; there are only a handful of people at Kimberly who moved from another state. One of our biggest problems was trying to find our way around the winding roads, all with similar names and abounding in charm—but the charm extends to the street signs, which are artistic, aesthetic, and virtually unreadable.

Some of our other immigrant problems were trying to find a liquor store (they are all state stores and there are very few), figuring out where beer is sold (nope, not at the supermarket, not at the liquor store); solving the mysteries of getting a driver's license, and reregistering the car (how were we supposed to know that "tags" had anything to do with license plates?), and registering to vote. We even had trouble finding our way around Kimberly Hills, which has non-consecutive apartment numbers and no maps or guides in the halls. We were only 200 miles from home but agreed that we had had far less difficulty traveling in Turkey. We often felt as if we had landed not just in a foreign country, but on another planet.

We had some strong first impressions that were exaggerated, to be sure, and of course they didn't apply to every single person. But they *were* our first impressions, valid or not. All the men seemed to have first names that were last names, like Slade, Ewing, or Bascomb. They wore red or green golf pants and plaid jackets (or vice versa), while the women favored lots of pink and green flowers and were called Bitsy, Lolly, or Mibs. No one ever used a bad word, and no one had ever voted for a Democratic candidate. Assuredly, no one had ever been poor.

The people were very friendly and very *nice* but, to us New Yorkers, they seemed dismayingly buttoned-up. They also had a great deal in common that we didn't share. Many of them had known one another all their lives. They had gone to the same schools, attended the same churches, belonged to the same country clubs, and they had many similarities. They were much more proper, conservative, and formal than the ethnically, culturally, religiously, and politically diverse society we were accustomed to; this was a very homogeneous population and much to be admired for many reasons, but, we confessed to each other, we sorely missed the old New York sizzle. We felt different, too, because, unlike us, almost everyone had married (and stayed married to) a teenage sweetheart, many of the men had been in business, and very few of the women had ever worked outside the home. I had always had close women friends, including at least one to whom I could tell *everything*, and I badly wanted to tell a sympathetic friend how bereft I felt about retiring, how much I missed my clients, the clinic, and the intellectual stimulation my work brought me. Although I knew that I would find substitute interests in time, right then I wanted to moan and groan to a kindred spirit I hadn't yet found (but would) at Kimberly.

Morton and I talked to each other all the time, sharing perceptions and feelings, wondering if we would ever lose the sense of being on a cruise ship and settle into some kind of real life. We were the new kids in school and knew that it would take a little time to tune into the culture and mores of the place, to learn the ropes, make some connections, and find our niche.

We were grateful every minute of every day that we had each other. It would have been much harder to do alone, although a great many widows and widowers do it with seeming aplomb. As mentioned earlier, most people have moved a distance of a few blocks or miles and have old friends at Kimberly and in the neighborhood. The majority of them also have children within easy visiting range so their family lives are not completely disrupted nor is the environment as foreign for them as it was for us.

But even if you lived next door, this is still a major move. You have left a home full of precious memories, given away many of your prized possessions, and become part of a small community with its unique culture and customs. The geography of the complex is unfamiliar and sometimes bewildering, and you can't imagine where you'll put all your stuff.

On that first day you may wonder if you made the right decision, but the answer is an emphatic YES—that is, if you have done your homework in advance. Before you move to a CCRC make sure you gather all the information you can so that you are fully informed and prepared to make a wise choice. Once that first upheaval is passed, you, like most others, will think it was the best choice you ever made.

CHAPTER 8

The First Year
and Beyond

E very CCRC has its own distinct culture and personality; each is
    different even from the one a mile down the road. You have prob-
    ably observed a similar phenomenon in groups of every kind,
from therapy or support groups and religious congregations to reading
clubs or secretarial pools. Why do people travel across town to attend
a church or synagogue because they feel it's better than the one of the
same denomination around the corner? Why is working for one insurance company so much more enjoyable than working at the same job
for some other insurance company?

The differences in group culture arise from differences in leader-
ship, the physical setting, the idiosyncrasies of the particular individu-
als who make up the membership, and a cognitive style that comes into
being early on in every kind of gathering and may then be perpetuat-
ed as a matter of custom. There are innumerable other factors, many of
them subtle and arcane.

A retirement community is no exception. CCRCs are particularly
complex societies, with unique dynamics that aren't necessarily immediately obvious. So, without clear clues during our early days at Kimberly, we were somewhat wary. Instinctively, we made a special effort
to keep a low profile, to fit in, to try to conform while we attempted to
figure out exactly what it was we were trying to conform to. But with
the passage of just a little time, we stopped being so self-conscious
and began to relax; as we grew more comfortable, we reverted more

and more to being our own plain selves just as we had always been. What a relief!

Here are some examples of what we were up against: Bridge is a very popular activity at Kimberly, and we were urged by almost everyone we met to join in the weekly tournaments. Although neither of us had played in many years and we both much prefer other kinds of interaction with people, we signed up. We weren't terrible (we even came in second one time), but we also weren't very good, it wasn't a lot of fun for us, and we often wished we were doing something else with the time. After a few weeks, we simply stopped going, and the world didn't end.

I came to Kimberly with only a few dresses. In my old town I generally wore suits for work and pants or skirts the rest of the time. But here, dresses seemed to be the norm. Any number of women, being friendly and helpful, told me that the best place to shop was a particular dress shop in town that *everybody* at Kimberly patronized and that I absolutely had to go there. So off I went. The racks were filled with those pink-and-green flowered numbers I saw virtually all the women wearing, and, as much as I wanted to conform, the New Yorker in me rebelled. After stressing over the choices a bit, I finally managed to find two relatively low-key dresses, bought them, hated them, wore each one once, then gave them away. Back to suits, pants, and a couple of basic black dresses for special occasions. I was becoming myself again.

While we were dealing with these little crises of adjustment, we were beginning to find a rhythm, a pattern of daily life that we found congenial. Having discovered early on that dressing for dinner every night was burdensome, and frequent visits to the dining room tedious, we fell into a pattern of going to the coffee shop with a basket and bringing home our dinner. I began to cook every Sunday, then more and more often (considered strange behavior here), and soon began to invite friends for dinner.

The usual way of entertaining at Kimberly, and at all the CCRCs we visited, is to have friends in for cocktails and hors d'oeuvres, then go together to the dining room. As newcomers, we received a number of invitations to do that, soon repaid some of them, and before long we had a circle of friends.

One of them quickly became a very special friend, a man with whom we felt great accord. He was a voracious reader, a writer and editor, and a lovable person. He lost no time in getting Morton and me to join the staff of the monthly newsletter, the first of our many volunteer jobs at Kimberly. Sadly and shockingly, within a few months of our meeting, this lovely gentleman died suddenly of a stroke. (In a community of elderly people, death is not uncommon and is one of the biggest downsides of living in any retirement setting. It's not easy to get used to, and perhaps one never really takes it in stride.)

Although we didn't realize it when we joined the staff of the Kimberly newsletter, that affiliation would soon play a major role in our lives. Within a few months, the editor retired and Morton replaced him. The simple newsletter turned into a hefty desktop-published magazine, complete with photos and illustrations. Morton has the equivalent of a nearly full-time job, which he loves, and I am a constantly busy staff member writing articles and reviews and assorted odds and ends for every issue.

In addition to my journalistic work, I have acted as volunteer facilitator of a support group. I am also a chairperson of a committee as well as an active member of several other committees. This kind of volunteer service is the backbone of CCRC life. The residents give of themselves unselfishly and generously and have a good time doing it. There is tremendous *esprit de corps*—a strong sense of cooperation; people are committed to acting for the common good, pulling together to make life as fine as possible for everyone involved.

Despite differences of opinion (yes, of course there are some; no population could possibly be as homogeneous as we had at first thought this one to be), people generally get along with one another here, and they are caring and supportive. The sick are visited, the bereaved are comforted and supported, and newcomers are called upon and invited to various functions and gatherings. Everyone turns out for the big community parties, and there are many of them. Every holiday, even the most minor one, becomes an excuse for music, dancing, entertainment, and good fellowship.

Worship services are very much a part of normal life here, and it is my impression that the vast majority of residents are active members of a church, synagogue, or other house of worship. Speaking just for ourselves, we find that church membership, aside from any spiritual considerations, gives us a much-needed second community, one that is largely populated by young families with children. It is vital for us to have links and connections to a society that includes people of all ages, and we go out of our way to enjoy many of the intergenerational events, parties, celebrations, and dinners at our church because they reassuringly link us to the larger world.

Speaking of dinners, we have always loved going out to dinner at restaurants, and here, in our new life, it is more important to us than ever before. We find it essential to get off the campus, to experience new places, see different people, and eat different food. Because Kimberly's dinners tend to be very American, we have sought out a number of ethnic restaurants—Greek, Indian, Italian, Mexican, Chinese, Thai—that give us a welcome variety of cuisines, are fun, and are generally not too expensive.

With the passage of time—it is over seven years since our move—we are completely at home here at Kimberly and well adapted to this different lifestyle. We don't miss having a house (except on big family holidays, and then we go to the children's homes instead) because we are still aware of all the responsibilities we used to have that we would find burdensome now. Our small garden at Kimberly requires relatively little labor (the staff rototills it each spring for us), but it produces all the tomatoes, squash, beans, and basil we can eat, and gives us fresh flowers throughout the summer and enough herbs to dry for the winter. Oh, and yes, we discovered that far from everyone is Republican and not all—or even most of—the men wear plaid pants.

Mysteriously, Morton and I don't ever feel confined, crowded, or in each other's way in our two-bedroom apartment. That may be due, in part, to each of us having good private office space, and in part to our spending so much of our time elsewhere in this spacious complex. We don't miss any of the possessions we disposed of either, but rather, feel a sense of liberation in being scaled down, the way it must feel to lose some extra weight.

Do I think Kimberly is perfect? No. But I think it's probably as good as it gets, and I think I might have reached the same conclusion had we moved to any one of a number of other good CCRCs—but I honestly don't know. There are a handful of things that bother me, and sometimes they bother me a lot. I haven't completely adjusted to the lack of democratic process—of being the ward of a board of trustees and an administration I didn't help elect. They are all presumably good, caring people who have my best interest at heart, yet I have always cherished the privilege of having a hand in choosing the people who govern me.

I am unhappy about the stiff increases in our monthly maintenance fee the last few years, a time of very low inflation (except for healthcare costs); I am displeased (and puzzled by) an arbitrarily set annual dollar cap on prescription drug costs that is much too low to be of much value and that (it seems to me) contravenes our original guarantees of prescription coverage. The language in our contract is murky on this point, and we probably should have paid more attention to that seven years ago.

So these are both philosophical and dollars-and-cents complaints, and they tend to interfere with my faith in the system to a degree. But my faith remains unshaken that a CCRC is still the best solution to dealing with the perils of life's closing years. To date, I haven't thought of any other that even comes close.

Although I am grumbling, I am glad to be here. I love having friends and acquaintanaces around when I feel social, I value the convenience of seeing my doctor right on the premises, of knowing that there is always a nurse on call if something goes wrong, of knowing that we will both be taken care of if we can't care for ourselves, and that our children won't have to give up their lives to ease ours. In fact, the full value of living in a CCRC was underscored and dramatized for me when the unthinkable happened—I was in a serious car accident. My experience is described in "An Unexpected Affirmation" on page 80.

Although our children probably don't realize it, coming here was a bigger gift to them than any other we could have given them. They know we are safe, they don't have to come running when we aren't feeling well, they won't ever have to take us into their homes or struggle with painful nursing-home decisions when we are near the end of life. We have even sent each of our children an important document, Directive to Heirs, which we update annually. This document tells them where to find everything they will need when the second of us dies. A sample of the information contained in the Directive to Heirs

AN UNEXPECTED AFFIRMATION

Only a few days after I had finished putting what I thought were the finishing touches on the first draft of this book, my life changed in a split second.

I had gone out on a sunny morning to do a few errands and was peacefully driving along a quiet suburban road, when suddenly—so suddenly that I never saw it coming or knew what happened—my car was struck squarely on the driver's door by a young man who ran through a red light. My car was totally destroyed, and I came close to sharing its fate; only the prompt action of the local police, who had me helicoptered to the Hospital of the University of Pennsylvania, saved my life.

I was very severely injured, having sustained a broken pelvis and ribs and massive internal injuries that required immediate extensive surgery. I was in intensive care for two weeks and in hospitals for many more.

My devoted husband was usually at my bedside by 8 AM and was there all day, driving a rented car back and forth into the city at rush hour. I believe that the ordeal was nearly as traumatic for him as it was for me. Our children, too, constantly journeyed back and forth from New York City to sit by my side. It was a grueling time for the entire family.

But after I had been hospitalized for close to two months, my doctors agreed to release me to the health center at Kimberly Hills because it could provide both the skilled nursing and the rehabilitative physical therapy I would require. The alternative would have been a rehabilitation hospital an hour's drive from Kimberly.

What a joyous homecoming I had! Even though I was housed in the health center, not in my apartment, I was on the Kimberly Hills campus and that was *home*. I had a spacious private room, Morton could trot in and out (twenty-four hours a day) without long drives and parking hassles, friends dropped in to visit, and the children could make themselves at home in our apartment when they came. It was a very welcome relief for all of us.

I had some great nurses and excellent care and my doctor came nearly every day. Before long I started physical therapy (on the premises, of course), learning to walk with a walker, then with a cane. I was taught how to negotiate stairs and how to do exercises to improve my strength and balance. The occupational therapist taught me how to get around my disabilities in order to perform the important activities of daily living.

In a short while I was sent home—in a wheelchair, not an ambulance! A nurse visited me twice a day for the first few days to make sure all was well, my medications were delivered to the door, my physical therapy continued, and the occupational therapist had my shower outfitted with a chair and a handheld showerhead so that I could safely wash my hair. Little by little, my life began to return to normal.

That was more than three years ago, and I am fully recovered at last. The entire experience has been extraordinary in many ways, not the least of them the support I got from the Kimberly community. I was truly overwhelmed by the flood of cards, gifts, food, flowers, and letters that poured in. They conveyed the most sincere and heartfelt sympathy, empathy, offers of assistance, and proffering of prayers—all for Morton as well as for me. People here *care,* and it has made us feel as if we have a great extended, and very loving, family.

As far as professional care goes, I believe that the entire staff of Kimberly participated in my recovery with all that their skill and good will could provide. I owe more than I can express to their dedication and abilities.

When I started this book I had no idea it would end with a "proof of the pudding" experience, but no one can ever predict what life will bring. It isn't a surprise to me that CCRCs really work, but I'm happy to have my beliefs confirmed (even though it was a hard way to go about it).

can be found in Appendix B. Even if you're not ready to make the move yet, it's still a good idea to have such a document prepared.

So far, Morton and I are doing well, and feel pleased—and a little proud—that we had the foresight and courage to make this move. It was hard to do at the outset, and it turns out not to be perfect; still, if we had it to do all over again, we would do it immediately. And it would all be so much easier now that we know how.

Conclusion

After seven years at Kimberly Hills, I think back with amazement at how confused we were when we first began to make retirement plans. There seemed to be so many choices, and then, one by one, they all seemed wrong. The solution of a CCRC seems so obvious now that I have to remind myself that back then, in our early planning days, most people had never even heard of CCRCs.

Those who are planning now will find a wealth of retirement information on the Internet, in bookstores, and in libraries, so they will find it both easier and more confusing that we did. Retirement communities of all kinds have sprung up on every available tract of land, and some are very attractive.

But if you are attracted to living in a retirement community, think ahead to the difference between aging in a conventional retirement community and in a CCRC. Do you really want to make another move in five, ten, or fifteen years? Wouldn't you rather have exactly the same comfortable lifestyle in a luxury home, a town house, or an apartment that comes with the assurance that, no matter what happens to you or to your spouse, you will always be cared for and never be alone?

If you want an easy lifestyle and total security, then you will soon be looking at CCRCs. And if you happen to come to Kimberly Hills, please stop by and say hello.

APPENDIX A

Checklist for Comparing CCRCs

When you make your first visit to a CCRC, you will have a number of questions in mind—but will you remember to ask them all? And if you visit several communities, will you remember what you asked and which marketing director gave which answers? You probably won't—unless you keep a careful record. This checklist will make it easy for you. Take along a copy every time you visit a CCRC and jot down the facts. You will find them invaluable for remembering details and for comparing features of different CCRCs.

Name of CCRC

Address (attach driving directions)

Phone number

E-mail address

Fax number

Marketing director (name and extension number)

Status (non-profit or for-profit)

CCAC accreditation status

Type of contract (extensive, modified, or fee for service)

Style of buildings

Size of campus

Number of units

General first impression (rate 1 to 5 and explain)

Philosophy (attach mission statement)

Refundable deposit (amount; how much is refunded if you change your mind?)

Special mention (noteworthy pros or cons)

FIRST CHOICE LIVING UNIT

Style (house or apartment, model name or number)

Number of rooms

Square feet

Layout (attach sketch)

Light (exposure, doors, windows)

Kitchen (aesthetics, equipment, counter and cabinet space, pantry, pass-through)

Bathrooms (number, aesthetics, cabinet space, size)

Laundry (in unit or common? convenient, clean, and functional? coin operated or free?)

Closets (number, size)

Garage (one car or two? convenient?)

Entry fee (refundable? 100 percent or less? Is 50-percent plan available?)

Monthly fee

Waiting list (when will unit be available? how much notice will you get? if you turn down an available unit, will you keep your place on the waiting list?)

Bridge loan (available if needed? percentage rate)

ALTERNATE OR SECOND-CHOICE LIVING UNIT

Style (house or apartment, model name or number)

Number of rooms

Square feet

Layout (attach sketch)

Light (exposure, doors, windows)

Kitchen (aesthetics, equipment, counter and cabinet space, pantry, pass-through)

Bathrooms (number, aesthetics, cabinet space, size)

Laundry (in unit or common? convenient, clean, and functional? coin operated or free?)

Closets (number, size)

Garage (one car or two? convenient?)

Entry fee (refundable? 100 percent or less? Is 50-percent plan available?)

Monthly fee

Waiting list (when will unit be available? how much notice will you get? if you turn down an available unit, will you keep your place on the waiting list?)

Bridge loan (available if needed? percentage rate)

COMMON AREAS

General impression (space, decorative style, upkeep; rate 1 to 5 and explain)

Dining room (size, style, hours, dress code)

Dining-room aesthetics (decor, table settings, staff, flowers, etc.)

Wine (permitted in dining room? will waiter serve it?)

Food (quality, menu, number of choices, healthfulness, presentation; deduction allowed for vacations? no-meal plan available? cost of extra meals? credit for no-meal plan?)

Service (trained staff, quality of service)

Home delivery (if you are ill will meals be sent to your home? if you are not ill?)

Guest regulations (fee for guest meals? trade-offs for missed meals?)

Coffee shop (size, style, aesthetics, hours, dress code)

Food (same as dining room? good choices? quality?)

Service (cafeteria-style or served?)

Takeout meals (can you pick up meals to eat at home?)

Auditorium (size, aesthetics, comfort)

Library (number and types of books, hours, regulations; librarian on staff?)

Pub or cocktail lounge (is there a place to meet friends for drinks? are set-ups provided? canapés? can you leave bottles behind?)

Lounges (are there ample and attractive lounges where you can mingle with others?)

Fitness center (hours, type of equipment; trainer with good credentials on staff?)

Swimming pool (indoor or outdoor? size, aesthetics, hours, regulations, locker rooms)

Jacuzzi (indoor or outdoor? size, aesthetics, hours, regulations)

Tennis (on campus or nearby? rules, hours)

Golf (on campus or nearby? rules, hours)

Other sports (for example, bowling, billiards, croquet, bocci, or shuffleboard)

Organized programs (for example, exercise, water aerobics, or sports competitions)

Residents' gardens (assigned plots for residents' gardens? fenced in? water and large tools provided?)

Bank (on premises?)

Beauty/barber shop (on premises?)

Guest rooms (rentable guest rooms on campus?)

Special mention (noteworthy pros or cons)

HEALTH CARE

Wellness clinic (routine care on premises?)

Number of doctors, credentials

Hospital (rating and location)

Social services

Visiting specialists

Lab

Prescription drugs included?

Insurance required

Transportation to outside doctors and dentists available?

Comments

NURSING CENTER

General impression

Private rooms available?

Number of rooms

Number of nurses

Dining room

Lounge area

Alzheimer's unit?

ASSISTED LIVING

General impression

Apartments or rooms?

Staff

Comments

AMENITIES

Number of meals included

Number of meals available

Housekeeping services

Linen service

Residents' association

Residents' newspaper or magazine

Concerts

Lectures

Plays

Other entertainment

Art studio (instructor?)

Crafts studios (ceramics, woodworking; instructor?)

Extra storage space (location, size)

Religious services (on premises or bus to your choice?)

Trips

Transportation to shopping

Transportation to concerts and other places

Pet regulations

Committees

Volunteer programs

FINANCIAL AND BUSINESS

CCRC owner

Board members

Years in business

Financial stability

Table of fee increases

Bridge loans

Tax deduction

Imputed tax

Remarriage rules

PERSONAL CRITERIA

List other important items

APPENDIX B

Directive to Heirs

This appendix includes a list of suggested information to send to your children (or other heirs if you do not have children) once you have completed your move to a CCRC. Having this information on hand will make their tasks easier if they are faced with a critical situation. Update your directive and send copies to your heirs each year. (In the event of an emergency, your CCRC should have the names of your next of kin and their contact information on file.)

1. Your social security number.

2. The location of your Last Will & Testament, as well as the name, address, and phone number of the attorney who prepared it.

3. Your health directive, including the location and contents of your Living Will. (This document may have a different name in your state.) And the location and contents of your Health-Care Proxy. (This document names the person who will make medical decisions on your behalf if you become unable to do so.)

4. The name and phone number of your primary-care physician.

5. The name and extension number of the CCRC social worker.

6. The name and extension number of the resident affairs coordinator at the CCRC. (The title of this position differs from facility to facility, so provide the name and the extension of a CCRC staff member

who can assist residents and families with entry to dwelling, extra keys, packing, and moving arrangements.

7. The location of keys to your residence, cars, mailbox, storage area, safe-deposit box, and so on.

8. The location of your car(s) as well as the location of registration and certificate of title.

9. Information about your life insurance policy or policies, including policy numbers, death benefit, and beneficiaries, as well as the location of the written policies and the name and phone number of insurance agent.

10. Your banking information, including the location and account numbers.

11. Trusts—the name and phone number of the trust administrator.

12. A list of investments, including the location of any certificates that are in your possession as well as the name and phone number of your stockbroker and/or financial advisor.

13. The location of your safe-deposit box and the name of cosigner(s), if any.

14. Information concerning your CCRC entry fee. (Is your estate due a refund, either total or in part, of your entry fee? If so, how much will it be? Provide the location of the copy of your contract or agreement. Give the name and extension number of the CCRC financial office.)

15. Location of storage areas outside your dwelling. Provide combination for locks or the location of the keys.

16. Your wishes regarding organ donation. (Have you made any arrangements for organ donation? If so, what are they and where are the documents? If not, what are your wishes?)

17. Your funeral arrangements. (Do you have any funeral arrangements? If so, list funeral home, place, and details of service. If not, list preferences and wishes. Include cremation or burial, disposal of remains.)

Resources

The Internet is an invaluable tool for researching CCRCs. If you don't have a computer, get help from a friend, relative, or librarian. Direct links to individual CCRC websites, which have not been provided here, are very informative, but keep in mind that they were constructed by skilled professionals to grab your attention. There's also a chance that some of the information on the individual websites, such as availability and prices, may be out of date.

The following resources are listed in order of relevance and usefulness. When addresses and phone numbers are provided, you can write or call for further information.

The Commission on Accreditation of Rehabilitation Facilities and the Continuing Care Accreditation Commission (CARF-CCAC)
1730 Rhode Island Avenue, NW, Suite 209
Washington, D.C. 20036-3120
Toll-free: 866-888-1122
Phone: 202-587-5001
Website: www.CARF.org/aging
This is the site to check for CCRCs that are accredited by the Continuing Care Accreditation Commission. It offers comprehensive information on what accreditation is, the process and criteria for awarding it, and an excellent array of direct links to accredited CCRCs.

American Association of Homes and Services for the Aging (AAHSA)
2519 Connecticut Avenue, NW
Washington, D.C. 20008-1520
Phone: 202-508-9498
Website: www.aahsa.org

This is the best resource for information about and links to all CCRCs that are non-profit, whether accredited or not. From the Home Page, click on "Consumer Information," then click on "Homes and Services Directory," and browse the list of AAHSA members. You can search by state and zip code but, unfortunately, the CCRCs do not have a separate listing so you have to plod through a list of all kinds of facilities. However, if you know the name of a CCRC, you can enter it and get a direct link to its website. Most have photos and good information.

The AAHSA offers the AAHSA Directory of Members 2005 *in print for $45. This directory lists all members of AAHSA and includes, but is not limited to, CCRCs. More than 5,600 not-for-profit service providers are listed. Order directly from AAHSA.*

ElderNet
Website: www.eldernet.com

Offers a good, but incomplete, listing of CCRCs by state. Only about half the states are represented.

**Medicare—The Official U.S. Government Site
  for People with Medicare**
Website: www.medicare.gov

At this site, you can find out how good the nursing care is at a CCRC and how it compares to other CCRCs. From the Home Page, click on "Compare Nursing Homes in Your Area." This is information you won't find elsewhere.

Retirement Living
Website: www: retirement-living.com

Lists CCRCs in the Middle Atlantic states only. The details include costs, but these may not be up to date.

Seniorsites

Website: www.seniorsites.com

A good source of information about non-profit (only) housing, including, but not limited to, CCRCs. There are also links to national and state resources.

State Agencies on Aging

Most states provide useful information about housing and other age-related matters on the Internet. To find the website for your state's agency on aging, go to a search engine such as www.google.com and type in [THE NAME OF YOUR STATE] followed by STATE AGENCY ON AGING. One of the first few websites listed should give you a direct link.

ElderWeb

Website: www.elderweb.com

This site offers helpful information on various topics, including pertinent news and other matters of interest to seniors such as finance and law, and living arrangements.

About the Author

Bernice Hunt, M.S., has been writing since early childhood. She was an English major in college but took one year of physics after a lengthy discussion with her advisor who argued that "girls don't take physics." (Obviously, this was a long time ago.) She prevailed, and Physics 101 was her entrée to a first job as a junior physicist. That credit led to her career as the author of more than sixty science books for children and later, as children's science editor for a major publisher.

In midlife, she returned to graduate school to earn a dual master's degree in mental-health counseling and gerontology and worked as a psychotherapist until her retirement.

Bernice Hunt has lived most of her life in New York City and East Hampton, New York. She has three children, eight grandchildren, and two great-grandchildren. She now lives in a continuing-care retirement community near Philadelphia with her husband, writer Morton Hunt. The couple has co-authored two books, *Prime Time: A Guide to the Pleasures and Opportunities of the New Middle Age* and *The Divorce Experience*.

Index

entertaining at, 76
fees vs. household expenses,
18–19
narrowing your search for, 29–35
number of, 15
overnight visits to, 46–49
people likely not suited for,
25–26
planning a tour, 46
proliferation of, 14–15
residents, example of, 15, 23–24
searching for, steps to follow,
35–36
start-up, 34
understanding, 16–18
visiting, 45–58
Contracts, types of. *See* Extensive
agreement; Fee-for-service
agreement; Modified
agreement.
Co-op units, 17
Cost, as a disadvantage, 25
Criteria list, example of, 42–43

Dementia, active minds and, 24
Deposits, 52
Depression, Cynthia's experience,
10–11
Dining experience. *See* Food service.

Educational opportunities, 24–25
Elderly
health worries of, 6
and importance of peer
relationships, 22
U.S. population of, 5–6
with Alzheimer's disease, 6
Entertainment, 63
Entry fees, 16, 17, 18, 42
range of, 17
types of contracts and, 21
refunds, 16–17
Esprit de corps, 22, 77
Extensive agreement, 20, 21, 56
as criteria, 34–35

Extensive contract. *See* Extensive
agreement.

Fee-for-service agreement, 21, 25, 56
Financial footing, CCRCs and,
26–27
Financial formulas for acceptance,
26
Financial resources and disclosure,
as a CCAC standard, 32–33
Financial security, CCRC and, 22
Financial situations, examples of
acceptable, 26–27
Fitness center, 62–63
Floor plans, 39
Food service, 59–62
For-profit CCRC, example of, 31
For-profit vs. non-profit status, 30

Gerontology, 13
Governance and administration, as
a CCAC standard, 33
Group culture, 75

Health care
criteria, 34–34
CCRCs and, 20
routine, 56–57
unlimited, 20
Health center. *See* Healthcare
facilities, inspecting.
Health requirements for admission,
16
Healthcare contract, discussing,
56–58
Healthcare facilities, inspecting,
54–56
Hired companion, Lucille's
experience with, 11
Hobbies, 63
Home care, Lucille's experience, 11
House chores, 9
"House prisoners," 11
Household expenses vs. CCRC fees,
18–19

RETIRING RIGHT
THIRD EDITION
Planning for a Successful Retirement
Lawrence J. Kaplan

Used by the US Military Academy at West Point, Continental Airlines, McGraw-Hill Publishing Company, the United Federation of Teachers, and the N.Y.P.D., *Retiring Right* is fast becoming this country's most popular book on retirement. Now in its third edition, it is primed to become number one.

Written by Dr. Lawrence J. Kaplan, one of the country's leading experts in retirement planning, this practical book answers all your most important questions about savings and investment income, the Social Security system, and so much more. Each section covers an essential area of concern, including lifestyle issues such as working, leisure, and housing; long-term retirement funding, including savings and investments and pensions; day-to-day financial considerations such as budgeting and taxes; and life and health insurance; as well as preparing for the inevitable through estate planning, wills, and trusts. The information in this book reflects the most current regulations so that you can take full advantage of the latest tax laws to maximize your retirement income.

Through planning guides and worksheets, *Retiring Right* helps you apply successful retirement strategies to meet your individual needs. These guides allow you to evaluate your financial situation, select and implement the means by which you can achieve financial security, and chart your course towards a fulfilling and secure retirement.

About the Author

Lawrence J. Kaplan received his MA and PhD from Columbia University in New York City, and is Professor Emeritus of Economics at John Jay College of Criminal Justice CUNY. An authority in the field of financial management, Dr. Kaplan writes and lectures extensively on the subject of retirement planning.

$17.95 • 400 pages • 7.5 x 9-inch quality paperback • 2-Color • Personal Finance/Retirement Planning • ISBN 0-7570-0132-7

IRA WEALTH
Revolutionary IRA Strategies for Real Estate Investment
Patrick W. Rice with Jennifer Dirks

For decades, banks and brokerage houses effectively convinced us that IRA holdings can be invested only in stocks and CDs. Then, with the sharp decline in the stock market, most of us could only watch as our retirement savings lost their accumulated value. Few knew that there was a viable alternative that offered both safety and growth. That alternative is real estate. That's right. Contrary to what you may have believed, it is perfectly legal to hold real estate investments in an IRA account—and to enjoy unprecedented returns.

For nearly twenty years, IRA investment expert Patrick W. Rice has taught thousands of men and women his revolutionary strategies for using an IRA to create wealth based on real estate. In his new book, Mr. Rice shares these moneymaking strategies with you. He first teaches you how to turn your IRA into a self-directed account. He then details the many ways in which real estate products can make you rich, from buying rental houses and notes to building shopping centers. Mr. Rice offers a wide variety of strategies for both the aggressive investor looking for high returns, and the conservative investor interested in a steady stream of income—all tax-deferred or tax-exempt.

Although it may be a little late to avoid the volatility of the stock market, the lesson has been simple: Don't put all your eggs in one basket. Patrick Rice now offers you an entirely new basket that holds golden eggs for a bright and rewarding future.

About the Authors

Patrick W. Rice is the owner of IRA Resource Associates, a firm that offers expertise in investment real estate for self-directed retirement accounts. A member of the National Council of Exchangors, First Oregon NCE, and Real Estate Marketing Group of Oregon, he is also an investment columnist for American City Business Journals. A highly sought-after lecturer, Pat speaks at real estate conventions across the nation on the subject of IRAs and real estate.

Jennifer Dirks has covered personal finance and real estate issues as a staff reporter at *The Seattle Times, The Columbian,* and the *Vancouver Business Journal.* In 2001, she won the US Small Business Administration's Oregon "Journalist of the Year" award, as well as the national "Journalist of the Year" award.

$16.95 • 272 pages • 6 x 9-inch quality paperback • Personal Finance/Retirement Planning • ISBN 0-7570-0094-0

HOW TO FINANCE ANY REAL ESTATE, ANY PLACE, ANY TIME
Strategies That Work
James A. Misko

Ever wonder how real estate magnates become real estate magnates? By filling out mind-numbing mortgage applications? By making personal guarantees to their bankers? Hardly. For years, successful real estate investors have used nontraditional methods of securing funding. They have created effective money strategies that circumvent banks, yet result in profitable deals. Now, real estate professional James Misko makes these innovative techniques available to the general public in *How to Finance Any Real Estate, Any Place, Any Time.*

In this easy-to-use guide, Jim offers more than forty-five nontraditional ways to buy properties. These are not pie-in-the-sky theories, but proven strategies that will put the wraps on virtually any real estate purchase. In this book, you will learn how to turn your dwindling stocks into real estate equities, how to acquire land without money, and so much more.

If the only thing holding you back from buying your dream house or investment property is financing, maybe it's time to buy "outside the box" with *How to Finance Any Real Estate, Any Place, Any Time.*

About the Author

James A. Misko has been a highly successful real estate professional for over three decades. He is a Certified Commercial Investment member of the National Association of Realtors, and has served as an instructor for this organization. As a sought-after lecturer, he speaks at local, state, and national real estate conventions. He is also a published author, an outdoorsman, and one of the most creative investment and exchange brokers in the nation.

$17.95 • 224 pages • 6 x 9-inch quality paperback • Real Estate/Finance • ISBN 0-7570-0135-1

**For more information about our books,
visit our website at www.squareonepublishers.com**

FOR A COPY OF OUR CATALOG, CALL TOLL FREE 877-900-BOOK, EXT. 100